OCEANOPEDIA
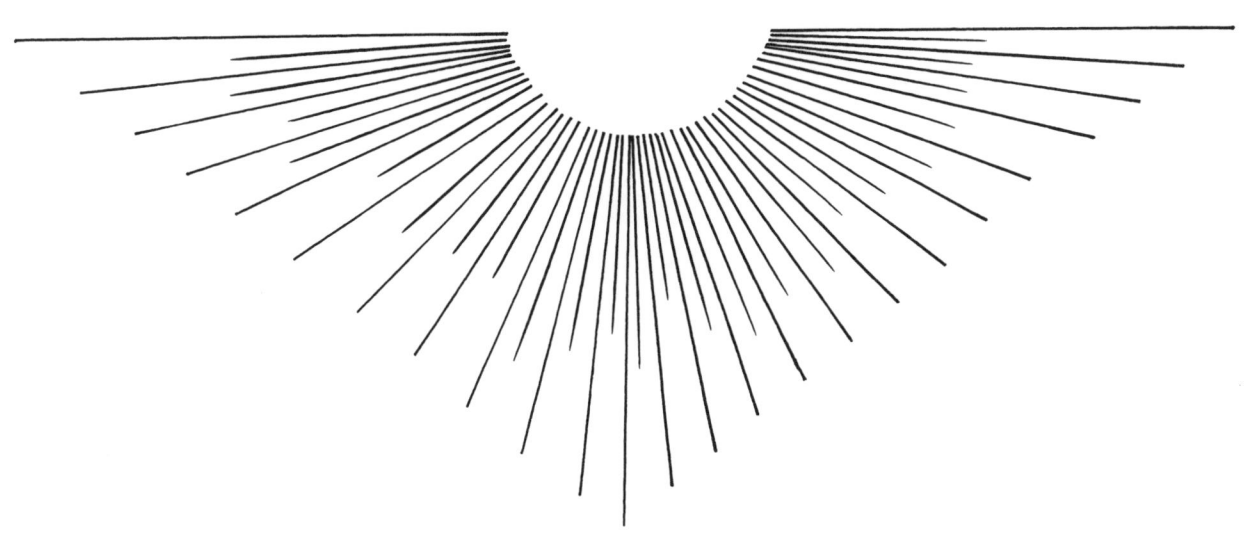

For Nara and Euan.
H.S.

As always, for my kids, Ernie and Bia, but also for my mum, who I hope lives long enough to see this book in print.
B.B.

To my water babies Tove and Kit, and also to all the good people, like Georg, working to restore and protect the oceans.
L.C.

LAURENCE KING

First published in Great Britain in 2025 by
Laurence King

Text copyright © Helen Scales 2025
Illustrations copyright © Good Wives and Warriors 2025

Helen Scales and Good Wives and Warriors have asserted their rights under the Copyright, Designs and Patents Act 1988, to be identified as the author and illustrators of this work.

All rights reserved.

No part of this publication may be reproduced, stored in a retrieval system, or transmitted, in any form or by any means, without the prior permission in writing of the publisher, nor be otherwise circulated in any form of binding or cover other than that in which it is published and without a similar condition including this condition being imposed on the subsequent purchaser.

A CIP catalogue record for this book is available from the British Library.

ISBN: 978-1-510-23124-5
Ebook ISBN: 978-1-510-23125-2

10 9 8 7 6 5 4 3 2 1

Printed in China

FSC® C104740 — MIX Paper | Supporting responsible forestry

Laurence King
An imprint of Hachette Children's Group
Part of Hodder and Stoughton
Carmelite House, 50 Victoria Embankment, London EC4Y 0DZ

An Hachette UK Company
www.hachette.co.uk
www.hachettechildrens.co.uk

www.laurenceking.com

The authorised representative in the EEA is Hachette Ireland, 8 Castlecourt Centre, Dublin 15, D15 XTP3, Ireland (email: info@hbgi.ie)

OCEANOPEDIA

AN ENCYCLOPEDIA OF
MARINE CREATURES

Helen Scales

Good Wives and Warriors

LAURENCE KING

CONTENTS

Our Ocean 7

ICY SEAS
Orcas 10
Antarctic Krill 13
Emperor Penguins 15
   Why Penguins Don't Live at the North Pole 16
Walruses 18
Narwhals 21
   How Not to Freeze 22

OPEN SEAS
Fin Whales 26
Floating Forests 29
   Our Plankton-Powered Planet 30
Neon Flying Squid 32
Portuguese Man o' Wars 34
Whale Sharks 37
Argonauts 38
   Who Goes the Furthest? 40

COOL COASTS
Puffadder Shysharks 45
   How to Be Flat 46
Weedy Sea Dragons 49
Rose Sunstars 51
Rainbow-Coloured Sea Slugs 52
Common Cuttlefish 55
   Dinosaurs in the Deep 56

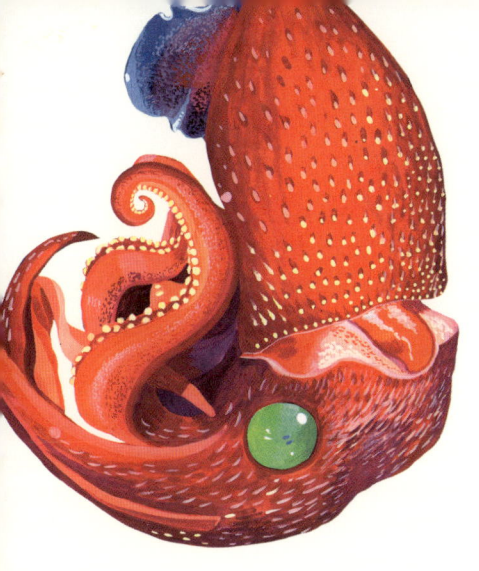

DEEP OCEAN
Strawberry Squid 60
Swimming Worms 63
Pearl Octopuses 64
   Glow-in-the-Dark Sharks 66
Fanfin Anglers 68
Psychedelic Jellyfish 70
   Life All the Way Down 72

TROPICAL COASTS
Rose-Veiled Fairy Wrasse 77
   Fish Are Smart 78
Peacock Mantis Shrimp 81
Angelfish 82
Bargibant's Pygmy Seahorses 85
   Coral Reef Teams 86
Magnificent Frigatebirds 88
Fiddler Crabs 90
   Our Changing Ocean 92

Glossary 94
A Final Note From the Author 96

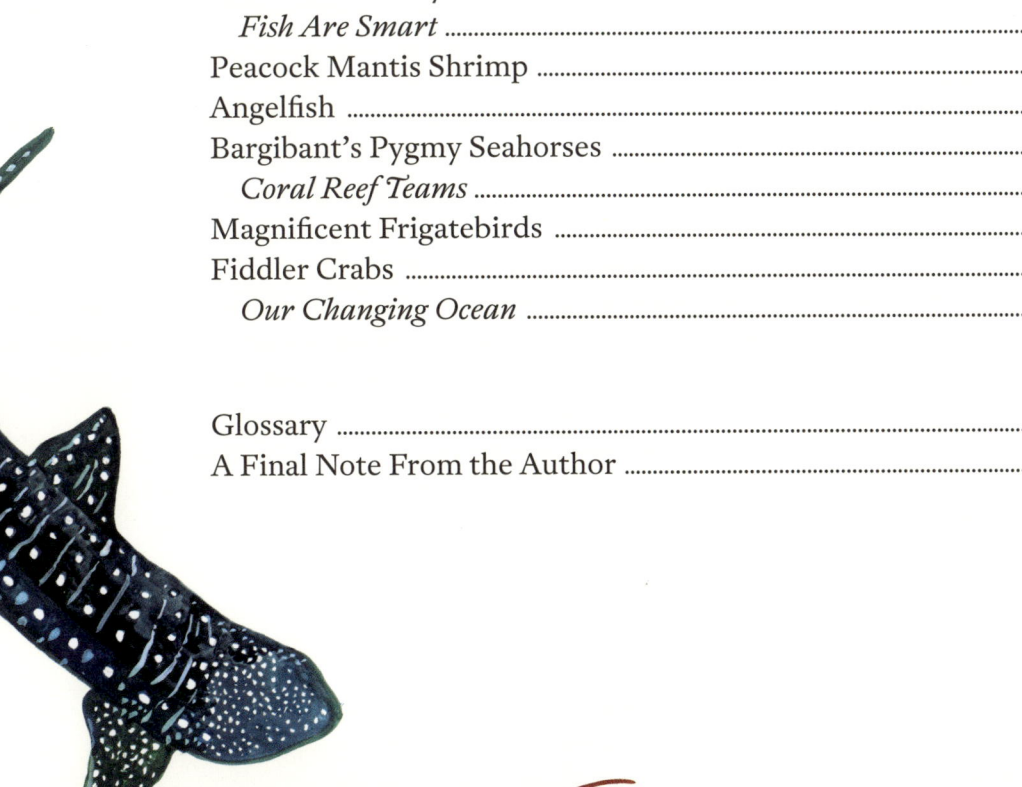

OUR OCEAN

The ocean is enormous. It covers roughly 70 per cent of the world. Instead of calling our home Planet Earth, maybe we should call it Planet Ocean! Particular parts of the ocean have names: the Pacific, Atlantic, Indian, Southern and Arctic, and smaller seas like the Caribbean and North Seas. These are all part of one single ocean that's connected by currents that flow around the globe like giant rivers.

The ocean is packed with mind-blowing creatures. Everywhere you look, there are tentacles and suckers, fins and flukes, bodies that are covered in spines or made of jelly and twinkling like stars.

This book is your guide to the ocean's amazing mix of life, showing you how to spot species and learn how they survive in many places, from the blue waves down to the dark depths.

Dive in and you never know what you might find!

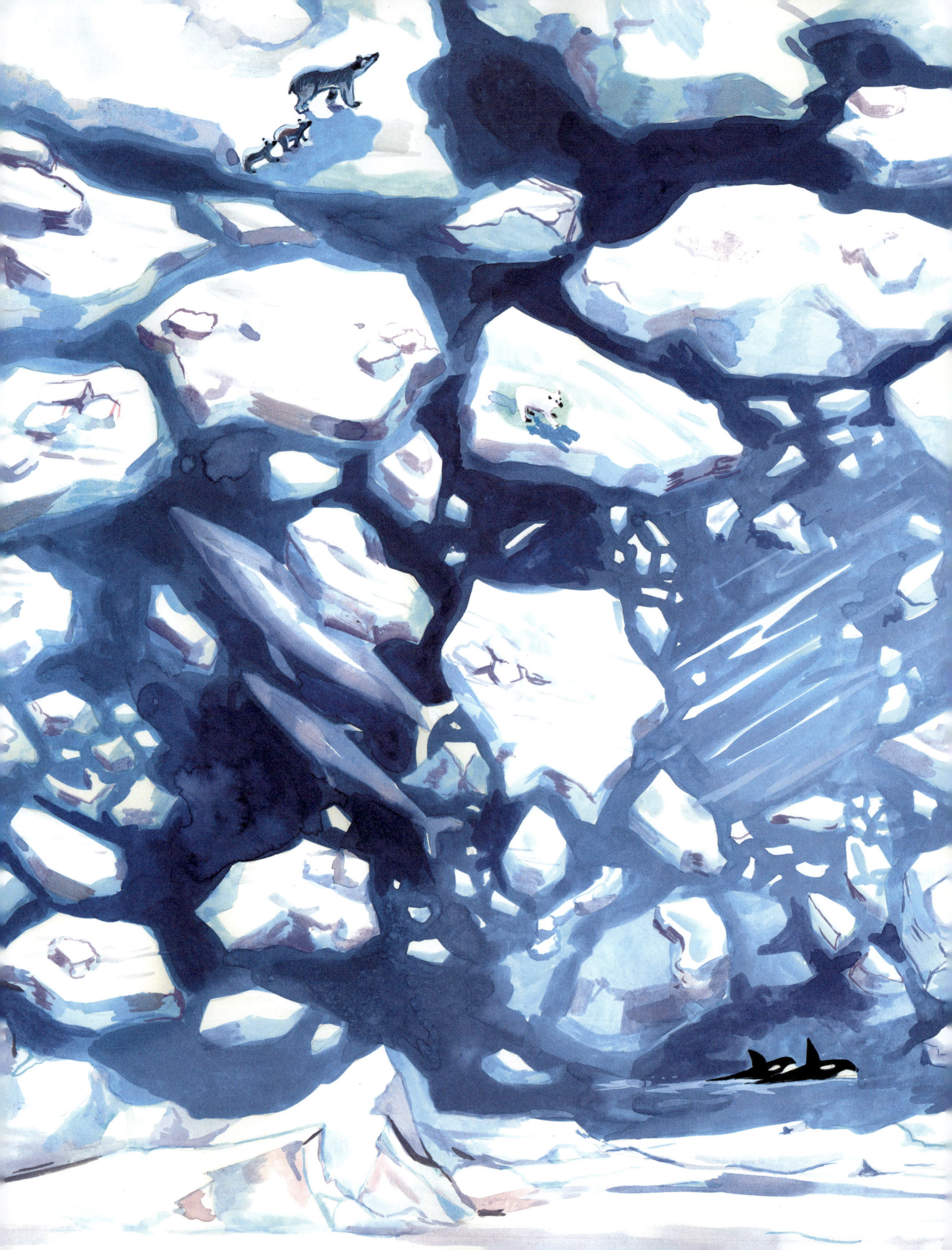

ICY SEAS

At the top and bottom of the planet lie the coldest, iciest seas. In the north, the Arctic Ocean is covered in a layer of ice and surrounded by frozen land. Down south, Antarctica is a continent covered in a giant ice sheet and surrounded by the freezing, swirling Southern Ocean. No country owns Antarctica – instead, it is left alone as a special place devoted to peace and science. The Arctic and Antarctic are both perilous places, but still many animals have found ways to survive there and make these icy realms their home.

ORCAS

Orcinus orca

Swimming through icy seas of both the Arctic and Antarctic are giant black and white predators, with tall dorsal fins that stand high above the waves when they come to the surface to breathe. These are orcas, the world's biggest dolphins, though you might know them as killer whales.

Orcas live in tight-knit family pods usually led by their grandmother, the wise elder who can live for up to one hundred years. She teaches young ones how to hunt and where to go. She protects her sons from getting into fights with other orcas and calls pod members to her with a splash of her tail.

Orcas live all through the ocean, including in warmer seas. Scientists studying orcas have learned they talk to each other with clicks, whistles and squeaks that are different around the world. An orca from the Arctic might not understand what an orca from Antarctica is saying! Orcas from different places also look slightly different and eat different things. In the Arctic, orcas chase after seals, sea lions and narwhals. The world's smallest orcas live in the Ross Sea in Antarctica, where they eat fish and have a distinct slanted white eye patch. Other Antarctic orcas eat penguins and minke whales, and some swim side by side, swishing their tails to create waves that overturn chunks of floating ice, tipping the seals that rest on them into the water. Orcas earned their 'killer' nickname for a reason!

ANTARCTIC KRILL

Euphausia superba

All around Antarctica live trillions of krill. They are crustaceans, distant relatives of shrimp, crabs and lobsters. Their transparent bodies have pink spots as well as dots that glow in the dark. You can tell if krill have been eating because their stomachs are full of bright-green algae, called phytoplankton, which they scoop up using their front legs as a net. Even though they're small (they grow about as long as your little finger), krill are vital for life in the Southern Ocean.

Most Antarctic animals eat krill. Albatrosses, petrels and other seabirds dive down to grab them from the sea. Crabeater seals swim through shoals of krill with their mouth open. They snap their jaws shut and squeeze water through their jagged teeth, which interlock like a sieve and trap the krill. Southern right whales, humpback whales, minke, sei and fin whales all come to Antarctica to sift krill from seawater with baleen plates, which are like enormous hairbrushes inside their mouths. In one day, an Antarctic blue whale can eat 3.6 million krill.

Eating lots of krill has a particular effect on many Antarctic animals – it makes their poo pink! When penguins rear their chicks on the white ice, their poos make colourful blots that can be spotted in photographs taken from satellites, which helps scientists count penguin colonies from space. Would you fancy counting pink animal poo?

EMPEROR PENGUINS

Aptenodytes forsteri

From the moment they're born, an emperor penguin's life is tough. No other animals survive Antarctic winters out on the ice. For months, the sun doesn't rise. Winds stir up blinding blizzards and temperatures plunge below -50 degrees Celsius (°C), which is much colder than freezers in a supermarket. But emperors are well prepared.

They start as an egg – the size of an Easter egg – balanced on their father's feet. He keeps his precious egg warm under a hood of soft, downy feathers and huddles with other emperor penguin fathers to share body heat. Eventually, the chicks hatch, the sun rises and their mothers return from hunting at sea. Male and female emperors take turns fetching food for their offspring. As the chick grows bigger and hungrier, both parents go fishing at once, leaving the fluffy youngsters to fend for themselves and practise huddling.

At four months old, the young emperor penguins are almost ready to march across the ice, dive into the ocean and fish for themselves. But first they must grow new feathers. They shed their down and sprout sleek feathers, forming a waterproof, windproof overcoat. Fluffy feathers underneath trap air and insulate them on long, deep dives. When they swim back up, a bubble trail streams from their feathers, helping them slide through the water and leap out. Penguins don't fly, but for a few seconds they can soar through the air. An animal with such a tough life deserves a fancy trick, after all.

Macaroni penguin

Chinstrap penguin

Why Penguins Don't Live at the North Pole

Kumimanu penguin

Emperor penguin

The Arctic and Antarctic are both extremely cold and icy but they are home to different mixes of species. Curiously, there are no penguins at the North Pole. Fossils show that around sixty million years ago, the ancestors of penguins lost their ability to fly through the skies and began flying underwater instead, using their wings as flippers. These first penguins evolved in the southern hemisphere and some were giants. Palaeontologists (people who study fossils of ancient animals) have found fossilised bones in Aotearoa New Zealand of extinct penguins that were as tall as people. Their name, Kumimanu, means 'monster bird' in the Māori language.

Penguins as we know them today didn't evolve until twenty million years ago. Their ancestors originally lived in Aotearoa New Zealand, then moved to Antarctica and evolved into the penguins that live there now. Only two species live all around the edges of Antarctica: emperor penguins, which are the biggest living penguins, and Adélie penguins, which are smaller. Chinstrap penguins look like they're wearing a black cap tied on with a band under their chin, while Gentoo penguins have a red beak and a white stripe

Adélie penguin

Gentoo penguins

between their eyes. Chinstraps and gentoos live along the Antarctic peninsula, a finger of land that points towards South America. They also live on several islands, such as South Georgia, as do macaroni penguins, which have spiky yellow crests on their heads.

Other penguins live in South Africa and South America. The most northerly colonies are in the Galápagos Islands, which are bathed in cool, food-rich ocean currents. Tropical seas form a barrier to penguins, because there's not enough fish and krill for them to eat in the warm waters. Also, penguins don't fly, so they can't set off on long journeys as other seabirds do.

Even if penguins did somehow reach the Arctic, they would face another big problem. They build their nests and rear their chicks on the ground or on the ice, which is safe in Antarctica where there are no land predators, but in the Arctic, nesting penguins would be in grave danger from polar bears and Arctic foxes. The Arctic's equivalent to penguins are seabirds such as puffins and little auks, also known as dovekies. These birds can fly and they build their nests high up on steep cliffs, safely out of the way. Fortunately for penguins, they can thrive in a place without prowling predators.

WALRUSES

Odobenus rosmarus

Among all the animals that live in the Arctic, one of the easiest species to spot is the walrus. For one thing, they're enormous – males can grow around 4 metres (m) long and weigh as much as a tonne. In their group of marine mammals, called the pinnipeds, the only species bigger than the walrus are the Northern and Southern elephant seals. Walruses are also quite easy to find when they hang out in huge herds of hundreds, either snoozing in a great big pile on a beach or lying on a platform of sea ice. A massive herd of walruses is very stinky and their fishy breath can be smelt from far away. Their favourite food are clams, which they find on the seabed using their sensitive whiskers. They suck the meat right out of the shells, like a vacuum cleaner.

Both male and female walruses have tusks. These long canine teeth help walruses haul out on to ice, and males like to show off their splendid tusks, waving them in the air as a sign that they are surely the finest, most powerful walruses of all.

Walruses live across the Arctic, from Alaska and Siberia to Canada, Greenland and Svalbard, but occasionally they're spotted further south. In recent years, several lone walruses have set off and toured the coasts of Europe, where local people have flocked to see these unexpected and magnificent visitors. Maybe they wanted to show off their tusks to new crowds!

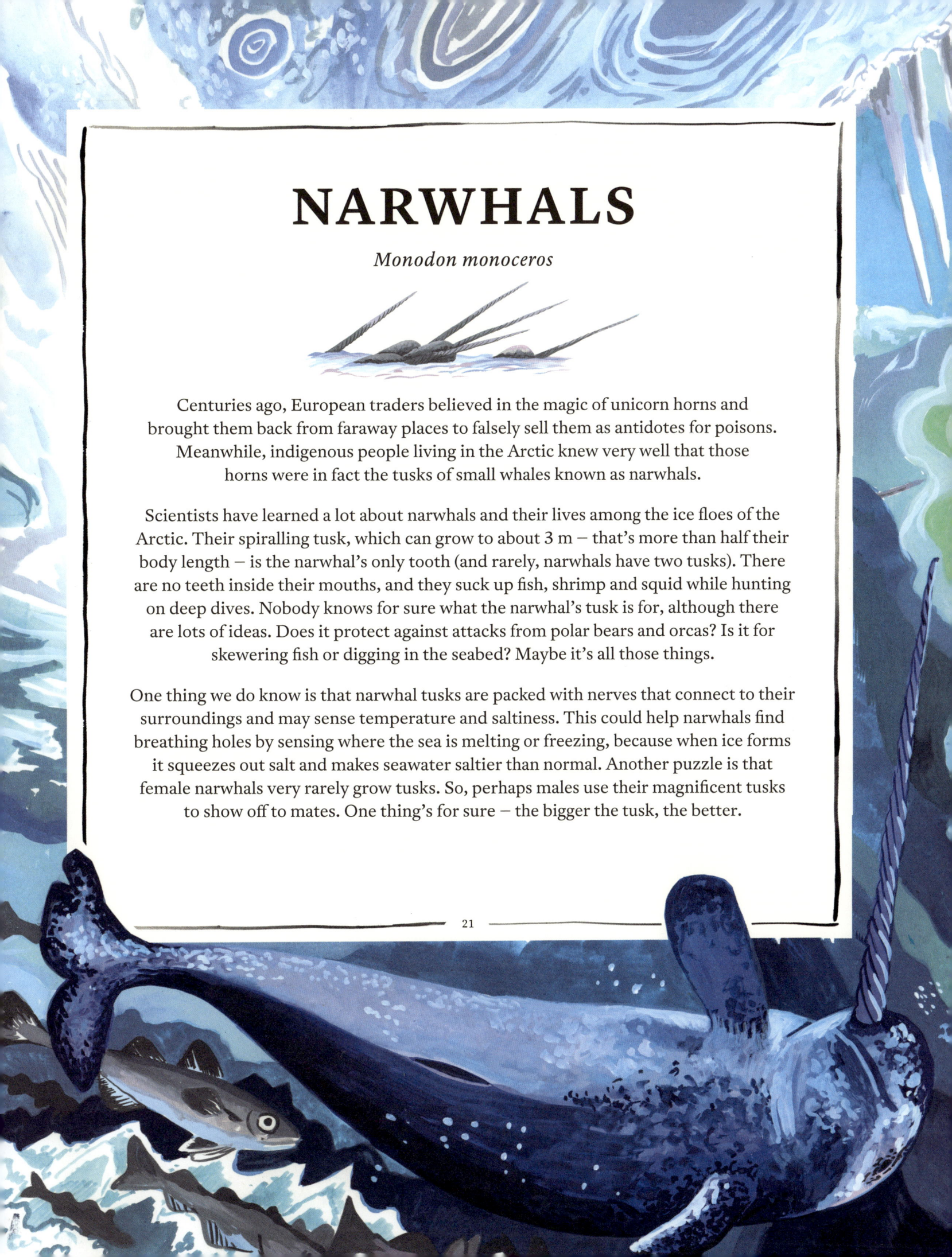

NARWHALS

Monodon monoceros

Centuries ago, European traders believed in the magic of unicorn horns and brought them back from faraway places to falsely sell them as antidotes for poisons. Meanwhile, indigenous people living in the Arctic knew very well that those horns were in fact the tusks of small whales known as narwhals.

Scientists have learned a lot about narwhals and their lives among the ice floes of the Arctic. Their spiralling tusk, which can grow to about 3 m – that's more than half their body length – is the narwhal's only tooth (and rarely, narwhals have two tusks). There are no teeth inside their mouths, and they suck up fish, shrimp and squid while hunting on deep dives. Nobody knows for sure what the narwhal's tusk is for, although there are lots of ideas. Does it protect against attacks from polar bears and orcas? Is it for skewering fish or digging in the seabed? Maybe it's all those things.

One thing we do know is that narwhal tusks are packed with nerves that connect to their surroundings and may sense temperature and saltiness. This could help narwhals find breathing holes by sensing where the sea is melting or freezing, because when ice forms it squeezes out salt and makes seawater saltier than normal. Another puzzle is that female narwhals very rarely grow tusks. So, perhaps males use their magnificent tusks to show off to mates. One thing's for sure – the bigger the tusk, the better.

How Not to Freeze

To survive in the icy seas around the North and South Poles, animals must avoid freezing to death. Pure water freezes at 0°C, but the salt in seawater allows it to get colder before it turns solid. In the Arctic and Antarctic, seawater contains so much salt, it drops to -1.8°C without freezing. This is bad news for cold-blooded animals because their body temperature matches their surroundings. They cannot fill their bodies with salt, so they need other tricks to stop them from turning into blocks of ice.

American marine biologist Art Devries was scuba diving in Antarctica several decades ago when he began to wonder why a species known as icefish doesn't freeze. He took some icefish back to his lab, extracted some of their blood and found that it only freezes at -2°C. Then he looked more closely at their blood and discovered their secret. Icefish make a kind of protein that acts as a natural anti-freeze. The protein traps ice crystals and stops them from growing bigger. The icefish then get rid of the trapped ice crystals through their poos. They also cover their bodies in slime that contains anti-freeze, which prevents them getting a frosty overcoat.

It turns out there's anti-freeze in all sorts of animals and plants, including plankton, moths, beetles, trees and lots more fish.

Crocodile icefish

Mackerel icefish

Jonah's icefish

Plankton

Arctic Cod

Arctic cod living around the North Pole have an almost identical form of anti-freeze as the Antarctic icefish, even though they aren't close relatives and they live at opposite ends of the Earth.

Birds and mammals are warm-blooded and generate heat inside their bodies. Their secret to survival in the Arctic and Antarctic is insulating themselves so they don't lose all their precious warmth. Penguins have layers of waterproof and downy feathers. Seals, sea lions and whales have thick layers of fat under their skin, called blubber.

Bowhead whales are the only baleen whales that live permanently in the Arctic. Their blubber is a whopping half a metre thick, which gives them such good insulation, they sometimes get too hot! When that happens, they open their mouths and let cold seawater stream in to cool them down. Walruses have a thick layer of blubber too. If the sun gets too warm when they're basking on land or ice, blood vessels open near their skin and radiate more heat, which is why a sunbathing walrus turns from brown to pink. Whether they need to cool down or warm up, these clever animals can keep their bodies at an ideal temperature.

OPEN SEAS

Over the horizon and far offshore from coasts and beaches lie the world's open seas. From above, they appear to be endless blue deserts, but take a closer look and they are full of life, from roaming giants to floating forests. Most species in the open seas never come near land or touch the seabed as they drift, swim and fly around the planet.

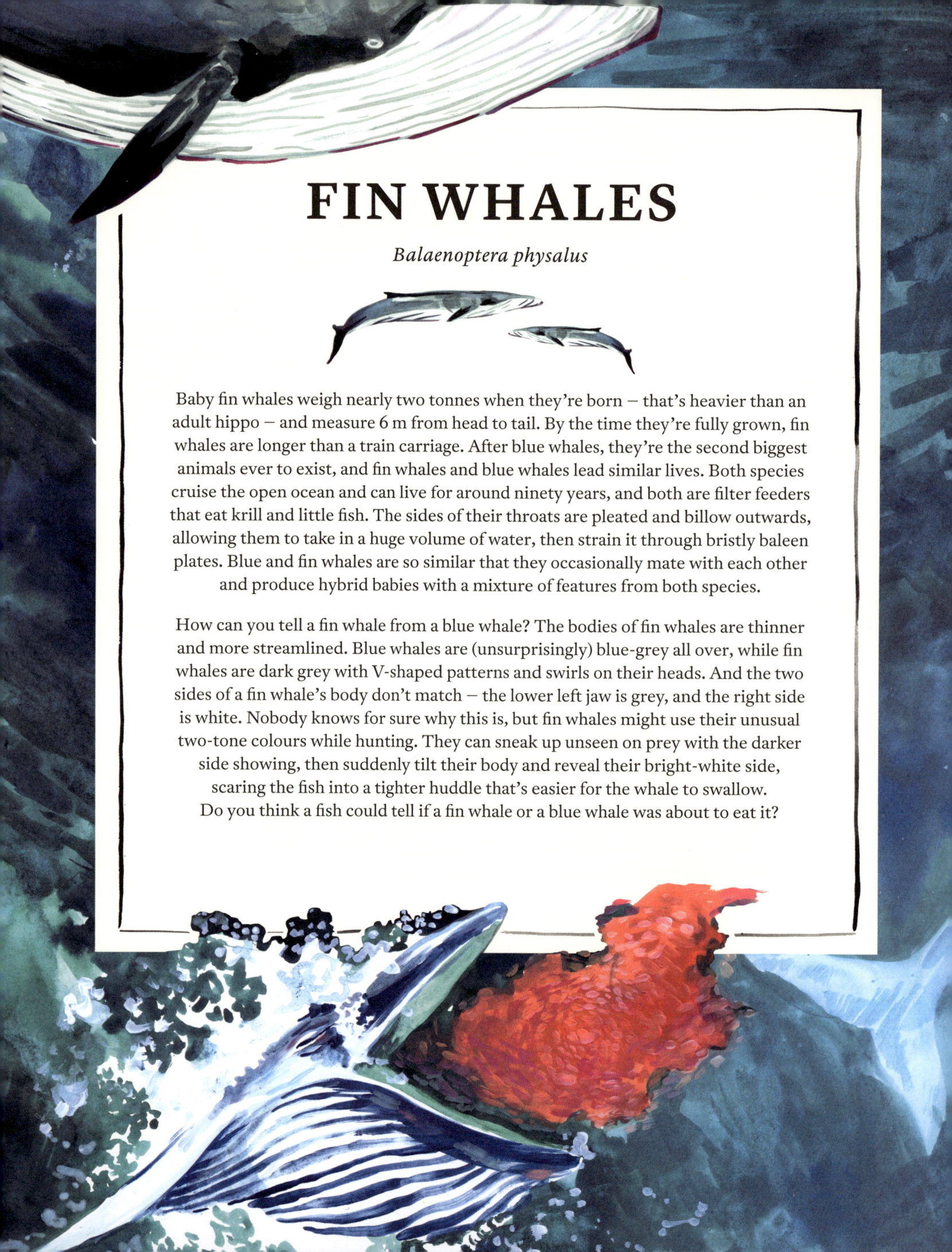

FIN WHALES

Balaenoptera physalus

Baby fin whales weigh nearly two tonnes when they're born — that's heavier than an adult hippo — and measure 6 m from head to tail. By the time they're fully grown, fin whales are longer than a train carriage. After blue whales, they're the second biggest animals ever to exist, and fin whales and blue whales lead similar lives. Both species cruise the open ocean and can live for around ninety years, and both are filter feeders that eat krill and little fish. The sides of their throats are pleated and billow outwards, allowing them to take in a huge volume of water, then strain it through bristly baleen plates. Blue and fin whales are so similar that they occasionally mate with each other and produce hybrid babies with a mixture of features from both species.

How can you tell a fin whale from a blue whale? The bodies of fin whales are thinner and more streamlined. Blue whales are (unsurprisingly) blue-grey all over, while fin whales are dark grey with V-shaped patterns and swirls on their heads. And the two sides of a fin whale's body don't match — the lower left jaw is grey, and the right side is white. Nobody knows for sure why this is, but fin whales might use their unusual two-tone colours while hunting. They can sneak up unseen on prey with the darker side showing, then suddenly tilt their body and reveal their bright-white side, scaring the fish into a tighter huddle that's easier for the whale to swallow. Do you think a fish could tell if a fin whale or a blue whale was about to eat it?

FLOATING FORESTS

Sargassum

Out in the open ocean, there are golden forests floating at the surface. They're not made of trees but seaweeds, called sargassum, that have little spiky leaves and round bubbles filled with gas that stop them from sinking. A large part of the Atlantic Ocean called the Sargasso Sea, which is 4 million square km and twice the size of Mexico, is named after the huge floating forests that are swept together by a giant swirling, clockwise current.

Just like forests on land, floating sargassum provides shelter and food for all sorts of creatures. Flying fish visit the forests to build bubble nests for their eggs among the seaweed. Shoals of young mahi mahi and swordfish swirl around the forests. After baby turtles have hatched on beaches and crawled into the sea, they go on long journeys and swim to sargassum forests where they hide, feed and grow.

At least ten species of animals live their entire lives in these forests and they're well camouflaged in their weedy homes. There are sargassum shrimp and crabs, pipefish and filefish, slugs and snails. Sargassum anemones look like little flowers, while sargassum frogfish are covered in weed-like fronds and can change the colour of their body in seconds to match their surroundings. And with so much living among the floating forests, it's no surprise they attract other predators too. Amberjacks and barracudas, wahoo and tunas are among the many hunters that visit in search of food. It's very busy in a sargussum forest!

Our Plankton-Powered Planet

The tiniest living things in the ocean are the most important. Without them, life in the ocean and on the whole Earth would be impossible because they make food for other things to eat and oxygen to breathe. To see them properly, you need a microscope, although sometimes there are so many, they paint the ocean in green and turquoise swirls that can be seen from space. Called plankton, which means drifters or wanderers, they're a mix of creatures divided into two main groups: phytoplankton and zooplankton.

Phytoplankton are miniature jewels of the sea. They can be circles or triangles, hexagons or stars, zigzags or spirals. And they all have one thing in common – they use the sun's energy to turn carbon dioxide into food. This superpower is called photosynthesis. Plants on land and seaweeds do it too. As well as making food, phytoplankton take carbon dioxide out of the atmosphere and actually produce half the oxygen humans end up breathing!

Many different types of phytoplankton live in the ocean. Diatoms are relatives of seaweeds that build glassy shells around themselves like fancy Christmas tree ornaments, while coccolithophores look a bit like golf balls, each one the same width as a human hair. The UK's White

Cliffs of Dover stand more than 100 m tall and were made from coccolithophores that lived and died 100 million years ago. Living coccolithophores release a chemical that wafts into the skies and causes clouds to form.

One very common type of phytoplankton was only discovered by scientists in the 1980s. They are incredibly small – a thousand of these miniscule green blobs would fit across a full stop. Called *Prochlorococcus*, they first evolved more than 2 billion years ago, long before most other living things. Today, there are 3 billion billion billion of them alive in the ocean. That's 3 octillion!

The second group of plankton are tiny animals called zooplankton. Some are larvae, which are the young stages of animals, like crabs and starfish, that often look completely different to the adults. Other types of zooplankton are tiny for their whole lives. Copepods are crustaceans with antennae and a single red eye, while sea butterflies are tiny snails that flit through the open water on little wings. Altogether, zooplankton form vital links in the ocean's food webs because they eat phytoplankton, which harness the sun's energy, then pass on this energy to bigger animals that eat them. These little animals play a big part in keeping our planet going.

NEON FLYING SQUID

Ommastrephes bartramii

All around the open ocean there are squid that fly. Sometimes shoals of a hundred or more squid leap out of the water at once and whizz along above the waves before dropping back into the sea. Neon flying squid grow to around 30 centimetres (cm), the length of a school ruler, and their bodies have a shimmering silver band. Other species fly too, including orangeback squid and Humboldt squid that grow to more than a metre long.

Squid flight has four phases. First is the jet-powered rocket launch. When they're swimming, squid suck seawater into a part of their body called the mantle, then squirt it out through a tube to push themselves backwards. They can also use their powerful water jet to break through the waterline; the squid folds its arms and pair of triangular fins against its body and launches into the air. During the second phase, the airborne squid spreads out its arms and fins into flat wings and carries on squirting a trail of water to push themselves along until there's no more water left. Next, it glides and soars through air. Finally, the squid folds away its fins and arms and dives head first into the water with hardly a splash.

Flying saves energy because air is much less sticky than water. And when they fly, squid can escape from underwater predators, although they do have to watch out for birds! There's no rest for a neon flying squid.

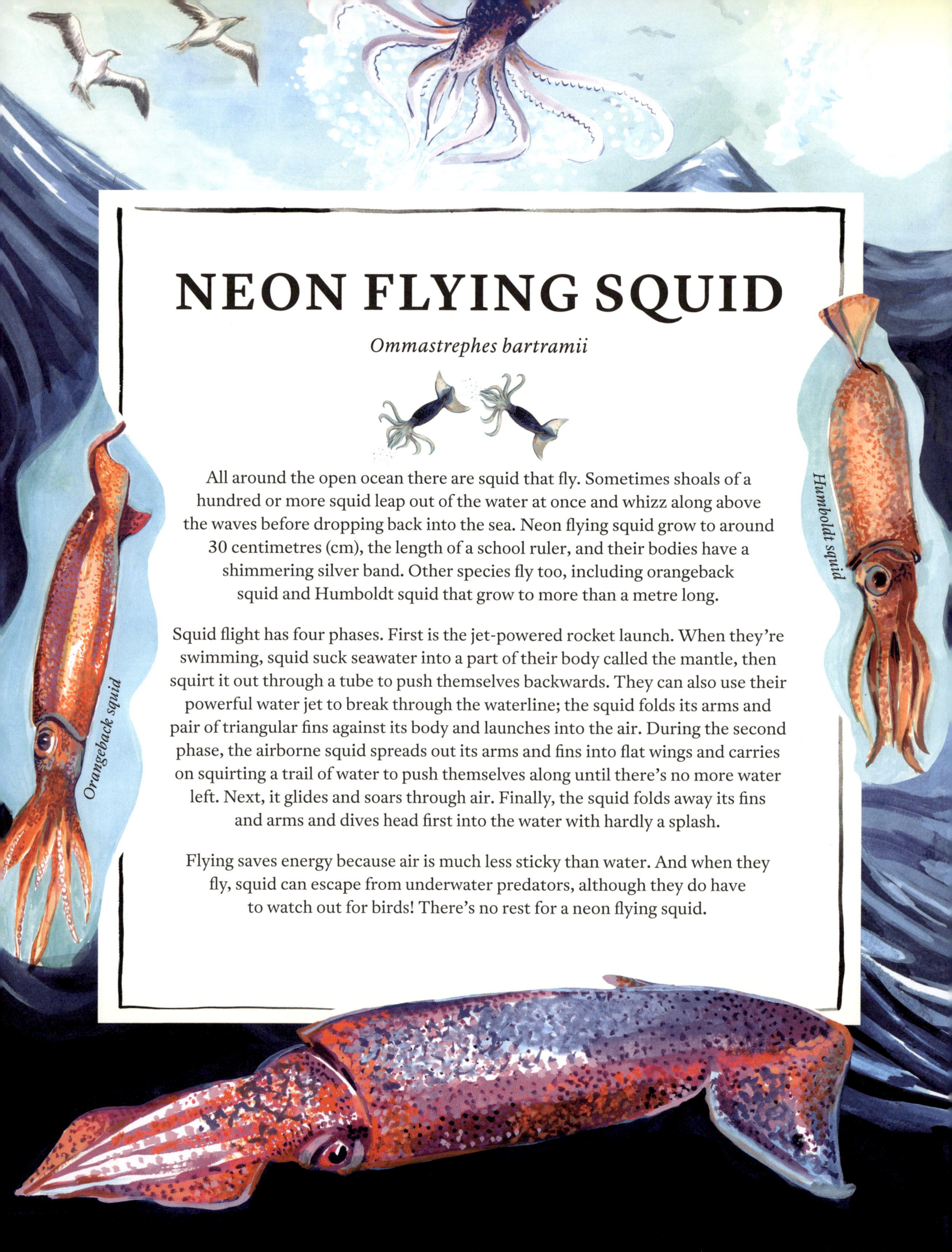

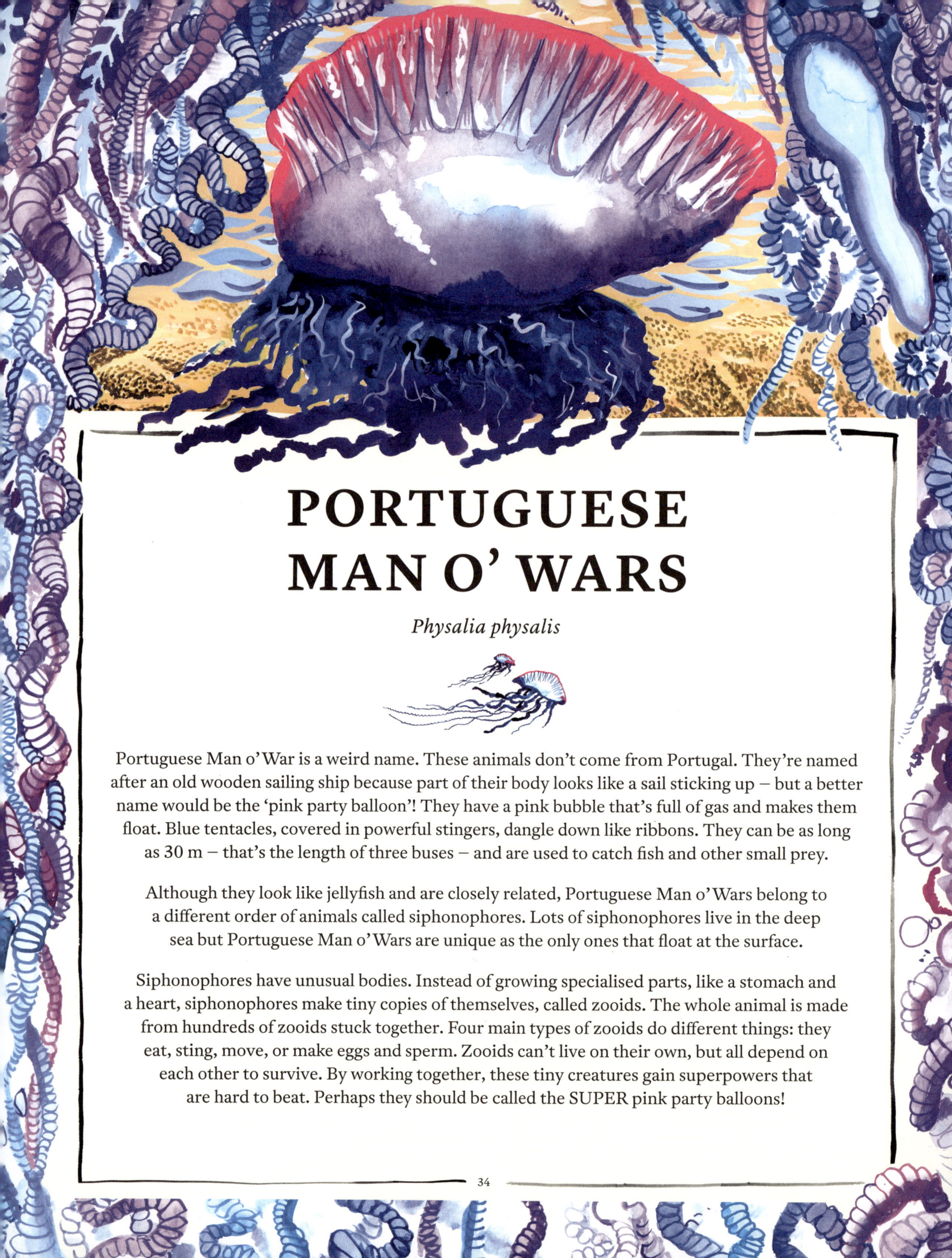

PORTUGUESE MAN O' WARS

Physalia physalis

Portuguese Man o' War is a weird name. These animals don't come from Portugal. They're named after an old wooden sailing ship because part of their body looks like a sail sticking up – but a better name would be the 'pink party balloon'! They have a pink bubble that's full of gas and makes them float. Blue tentacles, covered in powerful stingers, dangle down like ribbons. They can be as long as 30 m – that's the length of three buses – and are used to catch fish and other small prey.

Although they look like jellyfish and are closely related, Portuguese Man o' Wars belong to a different order of animals called siphonophores. Lots of siphonophores live in the deep sea but Portuguese Man o' Wars are unique as the only ones that float at the surface.

Siphonophores have unusual bodies. Instead of growing specialised parts, like a stomach and a heart, siphonophores make tiny copies of themselves, called zooids. The whole animal is made from hundreds of zooids stuck together. Four main types of zooids do different things: they eat, sting, move, or make eggs and sperm. Zooids can't live on their own, but all depend on each other to survive. By working together, these tiny creatures gain superpowers that are hard to beat. Perhaps they should be called the SUPER pink party balloons!

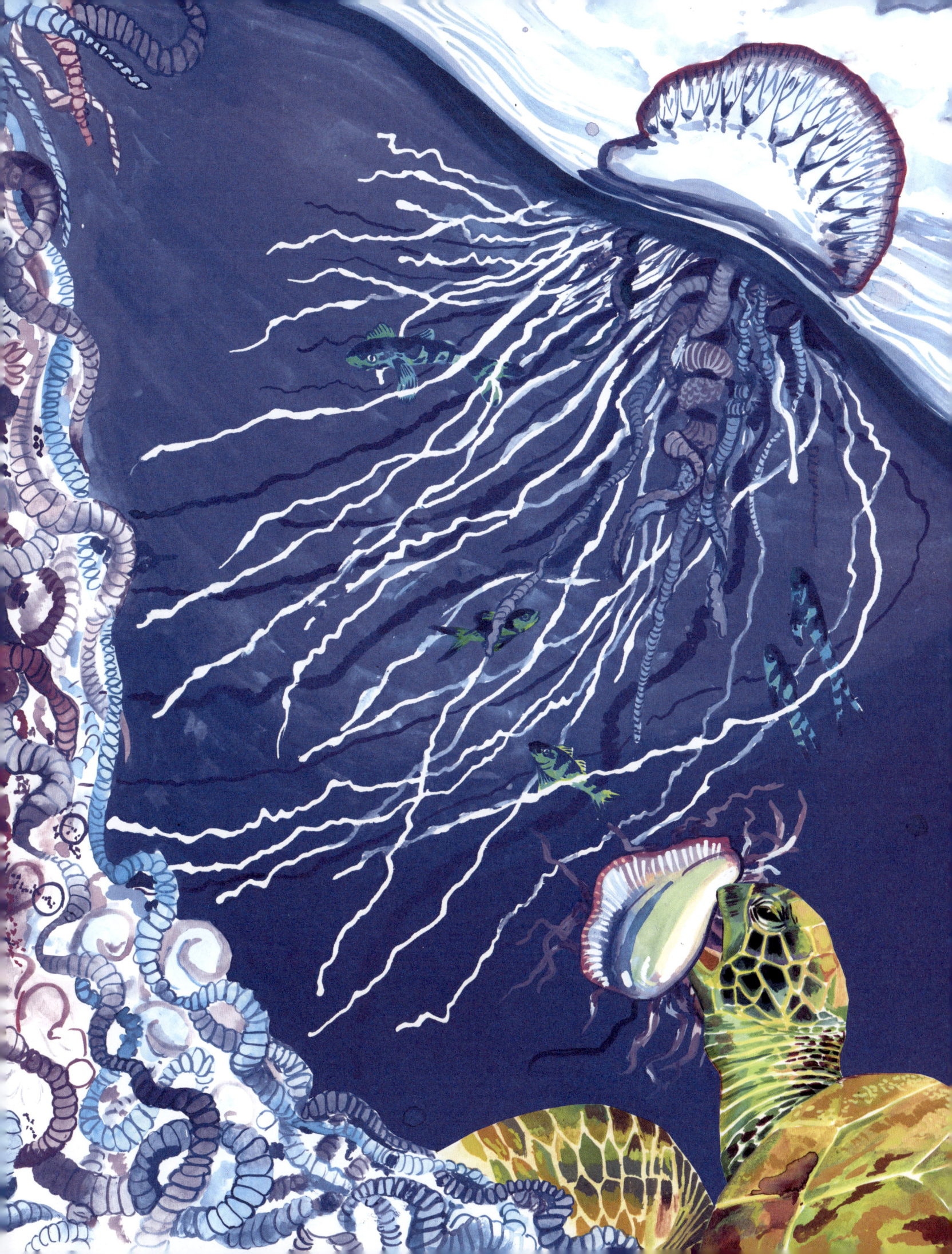

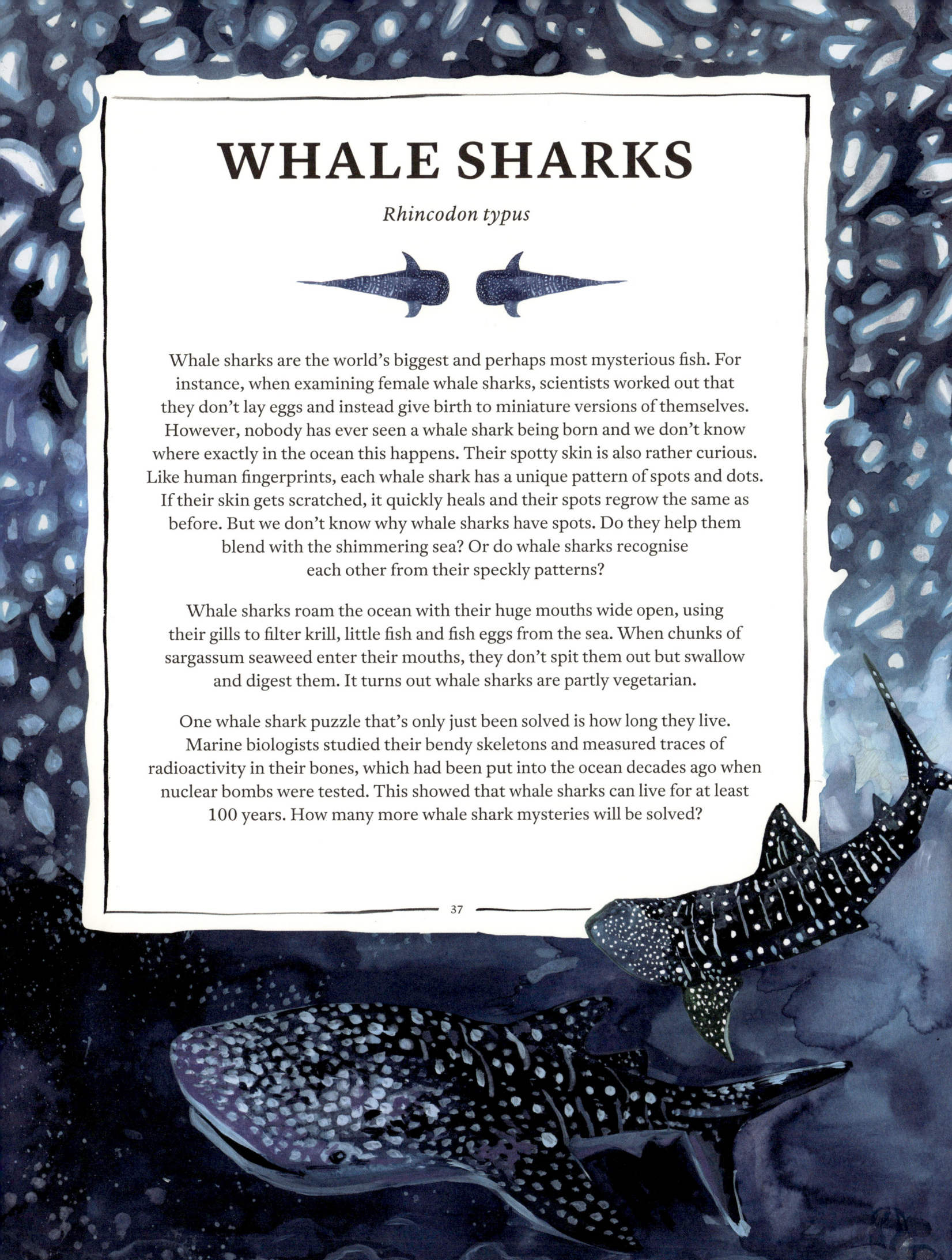

WHALE SHARKS

Rhincodon typus

Whale sharks are the world's biggest and perhaps most mysterious fish. For instance, when examining female whale sharks, scientists worked out that they don't lay eggs and instead give birth to miniature versions of themselves. However, nobody has ever seen a whale shark being born and we don't know where exactly in the ocean this happens. Their spotty skin is also rather curious. Like human fingerprints, each whale shark has a unique pattern of spots and dots. If their skin gets scratched, it quickly heals and their spots regrow the same as before. But we don't know why whale sharks have spots. Do they help them blend with the shimmering sea? Or do whale sharks recognise each other from their speckly patterns?

Whale sharks roam the ocean with their huge mouths wide open, using their gills to filter krill, little fish and fish eggs from the sea. When chunks of sargassum seaweed enter their mouths, they don't spit them out but swallow and digest them. It turns out whale sharks are partly vegetarian.

One whale shark puzzle that's only just been solved is how long they live. Marine biologists studied their bendy skeletons and measured traces of radioactivity in their bones, which had been put into the ocean decades ago when nuclear bombs were tested. This showed that whale sharks can live for at least 100 years. How many more whale shark mysteries will be solved?

ARGONAUTS

Argonauta

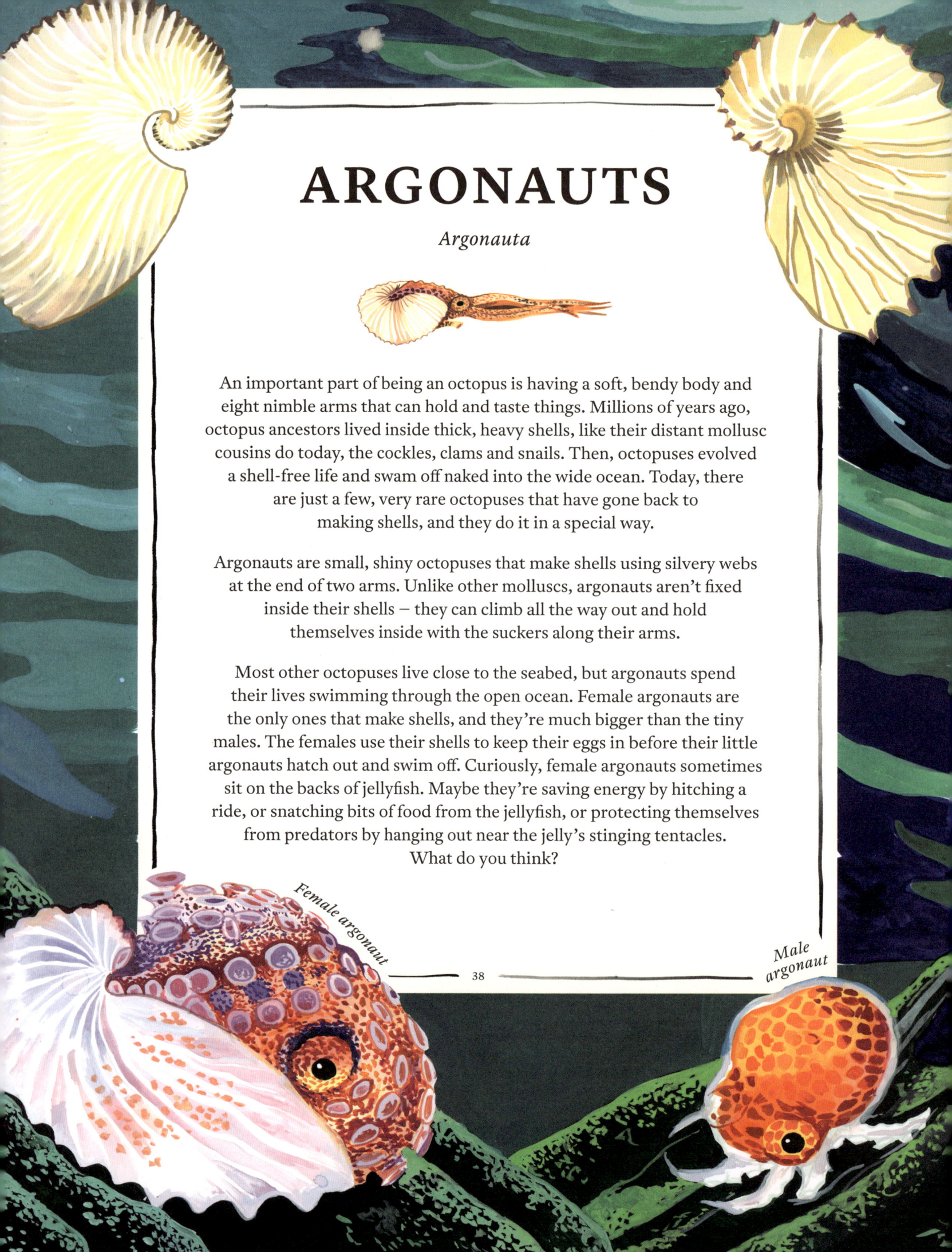

An important part of being an octopus is having a soft, bendy body and eight nimble arms that can hold and taste things. Millions of years ago, octopus ancestors lived inside thick, heavy shells, like their distant mollusc cousins do today, the cockles, clams and snails. Then, octopuses evolved a shell-free life and swam off naked into the wide ocean. Today, there are just a few, very rare octopuses that have gone back to making shells, and they do it in a special way.

Argonauts are small, shiny octopuses that make shells using silvery webs at the end of two arms. Unlike other molluscs, argonauts aren't fixed inside their shells – they can climb all the way out and hold themselves inside with the suckers along their arms.

Most other octopuses live close to the seabed, but argonauts spend their lives swimming through the open ocean. Female argonauts are the only ones that make shells, and they're much bigger than the tiny males. The females use their shells to keep their eggs in before their little argonauts hatch out and swim off. Curiously, female argonauts sometimes sit on the backs of jellyfish. Maybe they're saving energy by hitching a ride, or snatching bits of food from the jellyfish, or protecting themselves from predators by hanging out near the jelly's stinging tentacles. What do you think?

WHO GOES THE FURTHEST?

The ocean is enormous, and some animals see a lot of it during their lifetimes. Scientists fix electronic tags on to animals' bodies, which ping their locations to satellites and track where they go. Like a giant dot-to-dot puzzle, scientists then draw maps of the journeys looping around the planet, often between places where there's lots of food and other places that are good for spawning or rearing babies. But which animals go the furthest? And do they fly, float, swim or drift?

Several strong contenders have made epic treks of at least 20,000 km across the ocean — equal to halfway around the world. A great white shark called Nicole was tagged off South Africa and she crossed the Indian Ocean to Australia and back.

Anne the whale shark swam a similar distance across the Pacific. She started near Central America and travelled west towards the Mariana Trench, the deepest part of the ocean. A female leatherback turtle swam in the opposite direction, from Indonesia where she laid her eggs, to feeding grounds off the west coast of the United States. In the Atlantic, European eels travel 20,000 km, and for the first half of the journey they are tiny larvae!

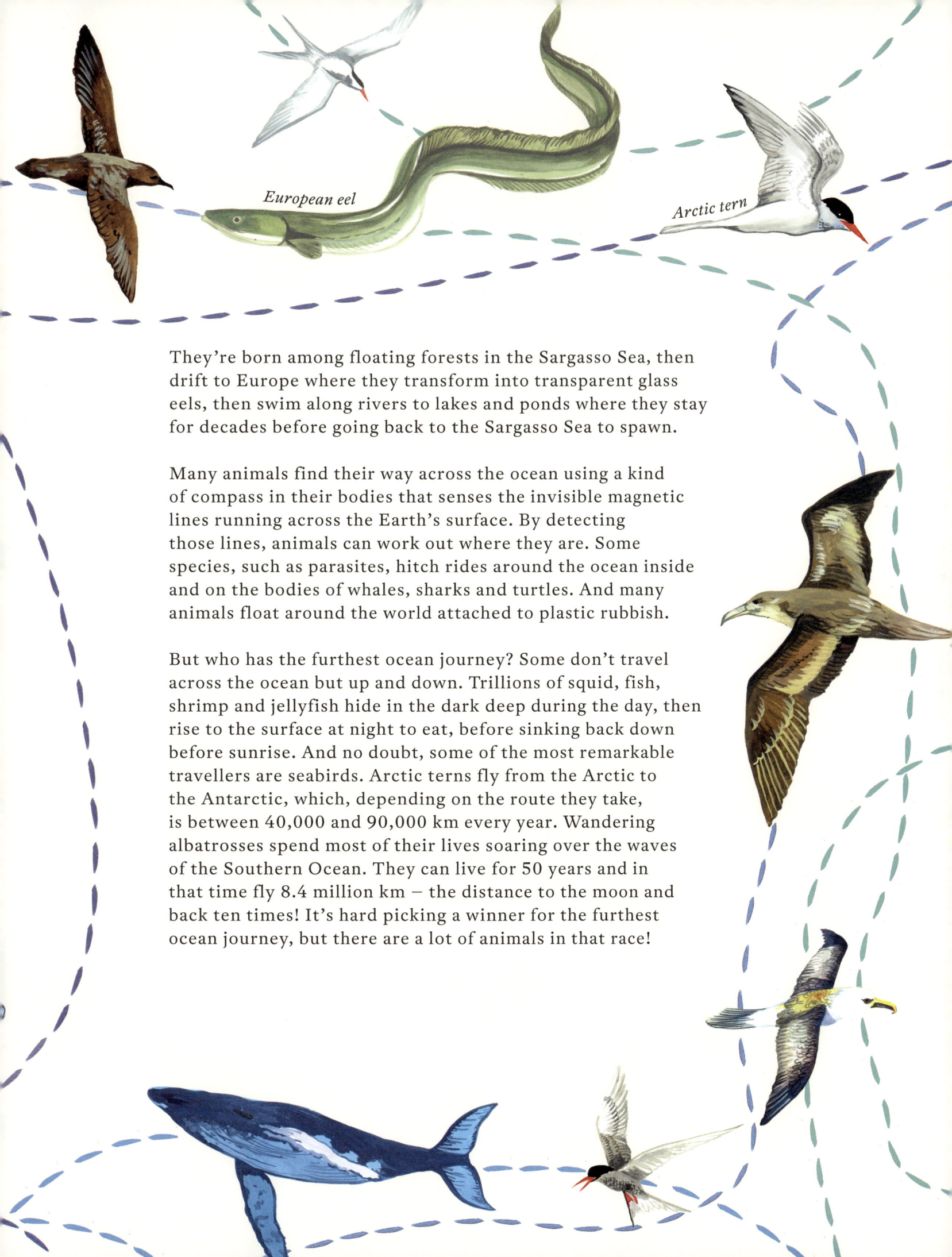

European eel

Arctic tern

They're born among floating forests in the Sargasso Sea, then drift to Europe where they transform into transparent glass eels, then swim along rivers to lakes and ponds where they stay for decades before going back to the Sargasso Sea to spawn.

Many animals find their way across the ocean using a kind of compass in their bodies that senses the invisible magnetic lines running across the Earth's surface. By detecting those lines, animals can work out where they are. Some species, such as parasites, hitch rides around the ocean inside and on the bodies of whales, sharks and turtles. And many animals float around the world attached to plastic rubbish.

But who has the furthest ocean journey? Some don't travel across the ocean but up and down. Trillions of squid, fish, shrimp and jellyfish hide in the dark deep during the day, then rise to the surface at night to eat, before sinking back down before sunrise. And no doubt, some of the most remarkable travellers are seabirds. Arctic terns fly from the Arctic to the Antarctic, which, depending on the route they take, is between 40,000 and 90,000 km every year. Wandering albatrosses spend most of their lives soaring over the waves of the Southern Ocean. They can live for 50 years and in that time fly 8.4 million km – the distance to the moon and back ten times! It's hard picking a winner for the furthest ocean journey, but there are a lot of animals in that race!

COOL COASTS

In between the hot tropical seas that surround the equator and the icy seas at the North and South Poles, cooler waters lap along the shores of temperate countries. These coasts are warm in summer and chilly in winter, but usually don't get very hot or very cold. This is where lush kelp forests, seagrass meadows and colourful rocky reefs grow, making homes for a rich mix of species.

PUFFADDER SHYSHARKS

Haploblepharus edwardsii

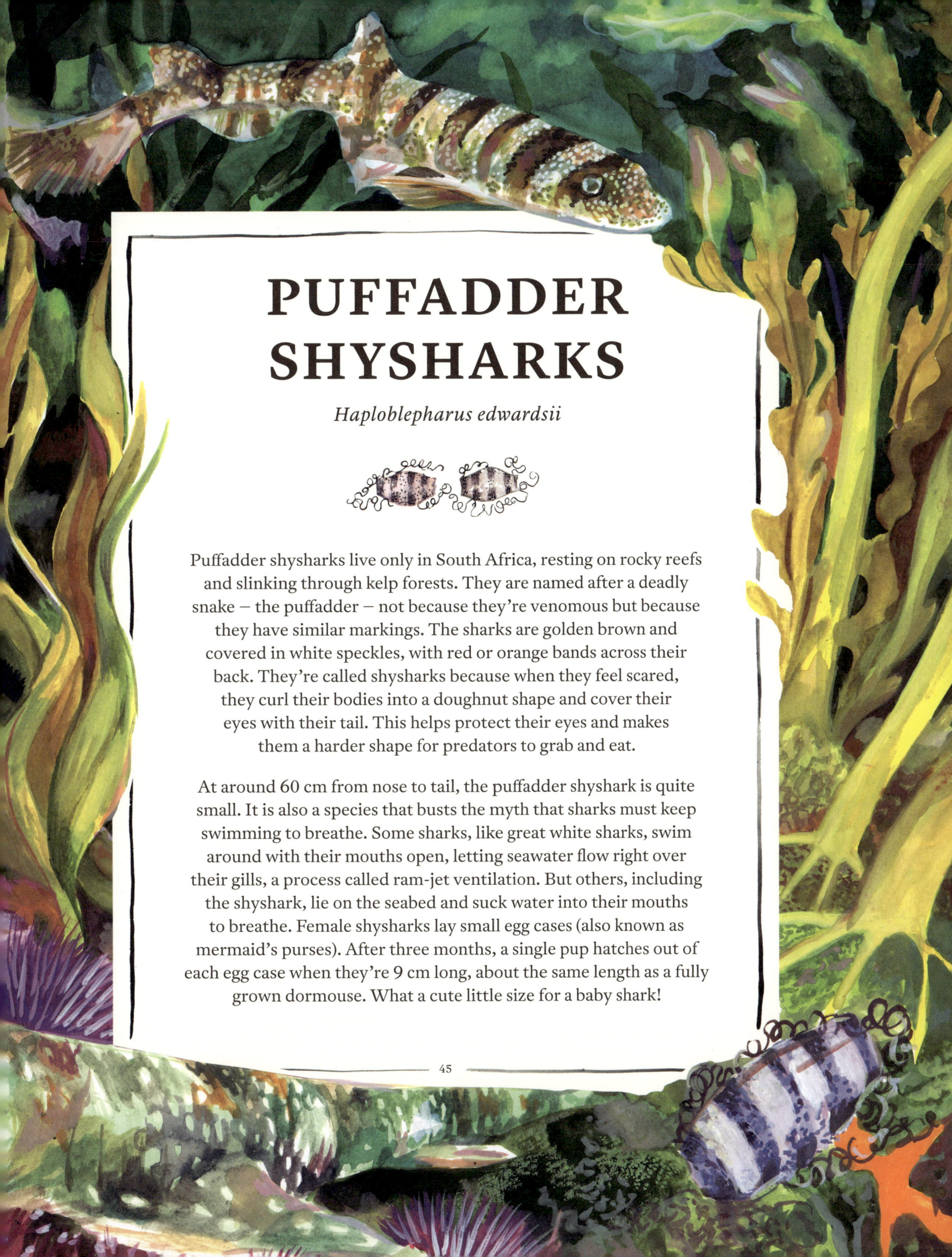

Puffadder shysharks live only in South Africa, resting on rocky reefs and slinking through kelp forests. They are named after a deadly snake – the puffadder – not because they're venomous but because they have similar markings. The sharks are golden brown and covered in white speckles, with red or orange bands across their back. They're called shysharks because when they feel scared, they curl their bodies into a doughnut shape and cover their eyes with their tail. This helps protect their eyes and makes them a harder shape for predators to grab and eat.

At around 60 cm from nose to tail, the puffadder shyshark is quite small. It is also a species that busts the myth that sharks must keep swimming to breathe. Some sharks, like great white sharks, swim around with their mouths open, letting seawater flow right over their gills, a process called ram-jet ventilation. But others, including the shyshark, lie on the seabed and suck water into their mouths to breathe. Female shysharks lay small egg cases (also known as mermaid's purses). After three months, a single pup hatches out of each egg case when they're 9 cm long, about the same length as a fully grown dormouse. What a cute little size for a baby shark!

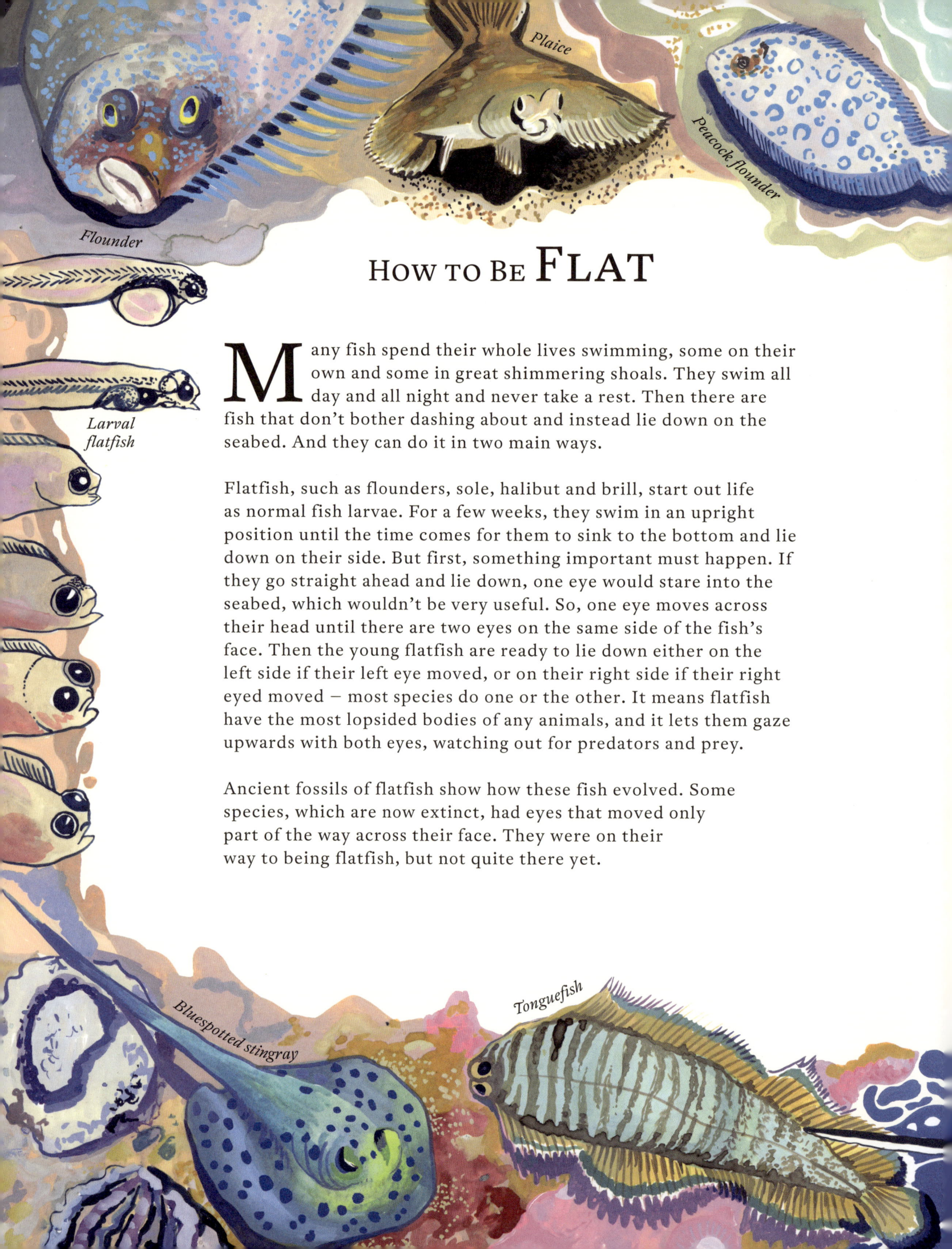

How to be Flat

Many fish spend their whole lives swimming, some on their own and some in great shimmering shoals. They swim all day and all night and never take a rest. Then there are fish that don't bother dashing about and instead lie down on the seabed. And they can do it in two main ways.

Flatfish, such as flounders, sole, halibut and brill, start out life as normal fish larvae. For a few weeks, they swim in an upright position until the time comes for them to sink to the bottom and lie down on their side. But first, something important must happen. If they go straight ahead and lie down, one eye would stare into the seabed, which wouldn't be very useful. So, one eye moves across their head until there are two eyes on the same side of the fish's face. Then the young flatfish are ready to lie down either on the left side if their left eye moved, or on their right side if their right eyed moved – most species do one or the other. It means flatfish have the most lopsided bodies of any animals, and it lets them gaze upwards with both eyes, watching out for predators and prey.

Ancient fossils of flatfish show how these fish evolved. Some species, which are now extinct, had eyes that moved only part of the way across their face. They were on their way to being flatfish, but not quite there yet.

After that, the first proper flatfish evolved. Scientists worked out that this happened 66 million years ago, around the time when the dinosaurs went extinct.

Lots of sharks and rays have also evolved to lie on the seabed, but they became flat in a different way to flatfish. Instead of lying on their sides, sharks and rays lie on their bellies. When they're born, their bodies are already squashed flat from front to back, and their eyes are already on the top or the side of the body.

Angel sharks have kite-shaped bodies. They hide on the sandy seabed, then they leap up and ambush prey that swims past. Stingrays have pancake-shaped bodies and swim by rippling the fins that wrap around their side. Some flat sharks and rays look a lot like each other. Sawsharks (a type of shark) and sawfish (a type of ray) both have long, flat snouts fringed in sharp teeth. To tell the two apart, look at their gills: sawsharks have gills on the side of their body, and sawfish have gills on the underside. Other rays, like manta rays and eagle rays, don't lie around all day like their ancestors did. Instead, they use their powerful flattened 'wings' to fly through the water. Being flat can be useful in many ways!

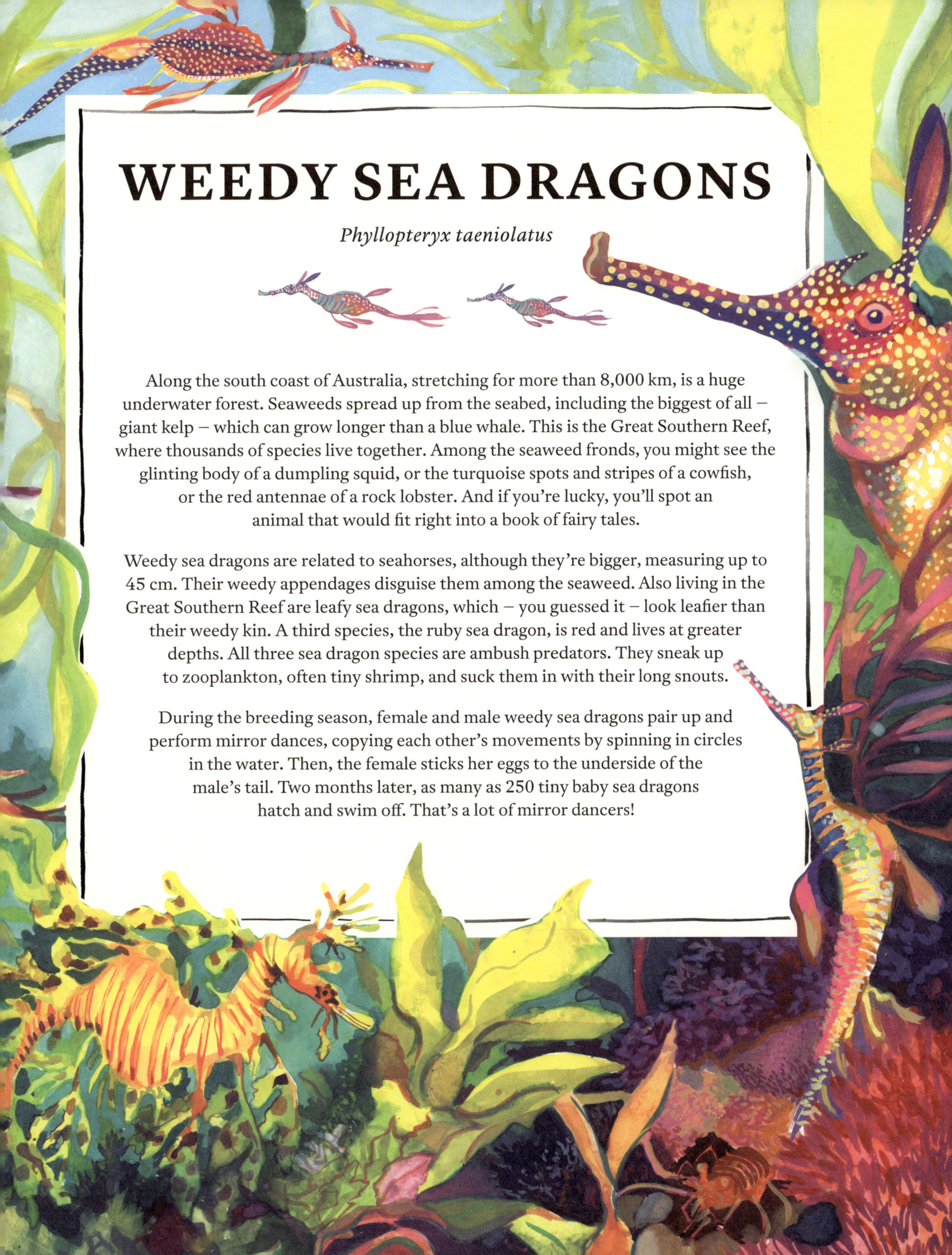

WEEDY SEA DRAGONS

Phyllopteryx taeniolatus

Along the south coast of Australia, stretching for more than 8,000 km, is a huge underwater forest. Seaweeds spread up from the seabed, including the biggest of all – giant kelp – which can grow longer than a blue whale. This is the Great Southern Reef, where thousands of species live together. Among the seaweed fronds, you might see the glinting body of a dumpling squid, or the turquoise spots and stripes of a cowfish, or the red antennae of a rock lobster. And if you're lucky, you'll spot an animal that would fit right into a book of fairy tales.

Weedy sea dragons are related to seahorses, although they're bigger, measuring up to 45 cm. Their weedy appendages disguise them among the seaweed. Also living in the Great Southern Reef are leafy sea dragons, which – you guessed it – look leafier than their weedy kin. A third species, the ruby sea dragon, is red and lives at greater depths. All three sea dragon species are ambush predators. They sneak up to zooplankton, often tiny shrimp, and suck them in with their long snouts.

During the breeding season, female and male weedy sea dragons pair up and perform mirror dances, copying each other's movements by spinning in circles in the water. Then, the female sticks her eggs to the underside of the male's tail. Two months later, as many as 250 tiny baby sea dragons hatch and swim off. That's a lot of mirror dancers!

ROSE SUNSTARS

Crossater papposus

Lying on the seabed off cool coasts in the northern Atlantic and Pacific Oceans are animals that look like a warm, glowing sun. Rose sunstars can grow bigger than a dinner plate and have ten to twelve arms that look like sunrays. They're a type of starfish, although they're not fish at all, but animals called echinoderms, which means 'spiny skin'. Other spiny-skinned relatives of sunstars are sea urchins, sea cucumbers and feather stars. They all build their bodies with an exoskeleton made of chalky plates called ossicles. Echinoderms move in a unique way using hundreds and thousands of tiny wiggling tube feet, which fix to the seabed with sticky slime. Scientists recently discovered that starfish arms aren't true arms and are more like extensions of their head, and a starfish's head is nothing like a fish's head. It doesn't have a brain, but a ring of nerves and its eyes are on the end of each arm.

Rose sunstars like to swallow whole other echinoderms, called brittlestars, which have five long, wriggling arms. Some parts of the seabed are covered in tangles of these bristly animals – there can be more than a hundred hand-sized brittlestars on an area of seabed the same as two open pages of this book. This is lucky for any hungry rose sunstars!

RAINBOW-COLOURED SEA SLUGS

Babakina anadoni

Compared to most slugs that live on land, sea slugs are much more colourful. One type of sea slug, *Babakina*, is 1 cm big, about the size of a fingernail, and it's neon pink, purple, orange and yellow. You might expect to see such a brightly coloured slug on a tropical coral reef, but in fact this species lives on cooler coasts.

Sea slugs are relatives of sea snails that long ago lost their shells. Without a hard covering to crunch through, predators should easily chew and slurp them, but sea slugs have other amazing ways to stay safe. *Babakina* looks like a feather duster and uses the 'feathers' along its back to breathe through and digest food. And if anything touches the tip of a 'feather', instead of a tickle, it gets a nasty sting. But sea slugs aren't creatures like jellyfish that have stinging tentacles. So how do they do it? Sea slugs steal stingers from their food! They eat sea anemones and tiny stinging creatures called hydroids without firing the stingers. Then the sea slugs move the stingers into their own skin, which defends them against attackers.

Other sea slugs eat sponges and corals that contain nasty-tasting chemicals. Without getting poisoned, the sea slugs store these chemicals in their skin, making themselves disgusting for anything else to eat. The sea slugs' bright colours can either match them to their colourful surroundings, making them difficult to spot, or the colours warn predators to leave them alone unless they want a mouthful of poison or stings. Being pretty is a brilliant way that sea slugs keep themselves safe!

COMMON CUTTLEFISH

Sepia officinalis

Cuttlefish are hard to see. They are masters of disguise and change the colour and texture of their skin to match their underwater surroundings. They hide from predators and sneak up on prey by pretending to be part of the sandy seabed or seaweedy rocks. Easier to find are the clues that cuttlefish leave behind on beaches. Cuttlebones look like miniature white surfboards, washed up by the tide. They're not really bones but internal spongy shells that cuttlefish use to control how much they float or sink underwater. Cuttlefish live for only two years and when they die, their cuttlebones float to the surface and easily get swept onto a beach.

More than a hundred species of cuttlefish live around the world and the one of the biggest is the common cuttlefish from the cool coasts of the eastern Atlantic Ocean and Mediterranean Sea. They can grow to the size and weight of an average pet cat. They have three hearts, blue-green blood and eight arms (with suckers all the way along), plus an additional pair of tentacles (with suckers just at the end) that shoot out and grab prey. Cuttlefish are highly intelligent too — baby cuttlefish can count and tell apart different numbers of shrimp. Cuttlefish also have amazing self-control. Scientists found this out by offering them either one treat now or a tastier snack if they wait a few minutes. Cuttlefish soon learn it's worth waiting!

DINOSAURS IN THE DEEP

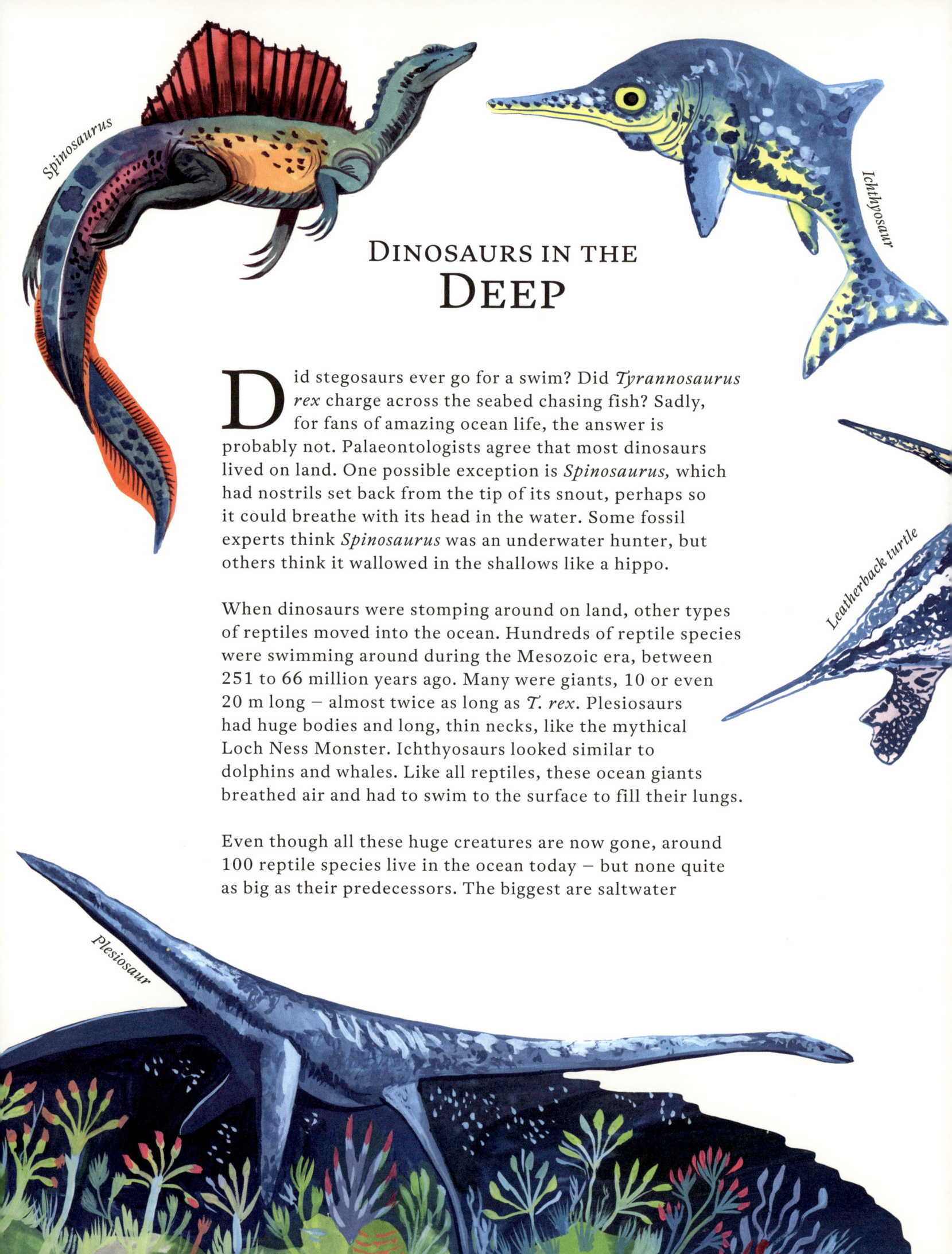

Spinosaurus

Ichthyosaur

Leatherback turtle

Plesiosaur

Did stegosaurs ever go for a swim? Did *Tyrannosaurus rex* charge across the seabed chasing fish? Sadly, for fans of amazing ocean life, the answer is probably not. Palaeontologists agree that most dinosaurs lived on land. One possible exception is *Spinosaurus,* which had nostrils set back from the tip of its snout, perhaps so it could breathe with its head in the water. Some fossil experts think *Spinosaurus* was an underwater hunter, but others think it wallowed in the shallows like a hippo.

When dinosaurs were stomping around on land, other types of reptiles moved into the ocean. Hundreds of reptile species were swimming around during the Mesozoic era, between 251 to 66 million years ago. Many were giants, 10 or even 20 m long – almost twice as long as *T. rex*. Plesiosaurs had huge bodies and long, thin necks, like the mythical Loch Ness Monster. Ichthyosaurs looked similar to dolphins and whales. Like all reptiles, these ocean giants breathed air and had to swim to the surface to fill their lungs.

Even though all these huge creatures are now gone, around 100 reptile species live in the ocean today – but none quite as big as their predecessors. The biggest are saltwater

Marine iguana

Marine iguana

crocodiles, which grow to 6 m and weigh a tonne. They live on coastlines in Australia, India and Southeast Asia and can swim long distances through the open sea. In the Galápagos Islands, marine iguanas are the only lizards that dive into the ocean. They chew on seaweeds, then climb out to warm up in the sun.

Sea turtles first evolved in the Mesozoic and were eaten by ichthyosaurs and mosasaurs. The largest ever sea turtle, *Archelon*, lived in this era, and it was close to 5 m long, more than twice the size of the largest living species, the leatherback turtle. Six other sea turtle species are alive today. Green, loggerhead and hawksbill turtles swim through the world's warm seas. Flatback turtles live only in Australia. The two smallest species, the length of two school rulers (60 cm), are olive ridley and Kemp's ridley sea turtles. Sea turtles sleep on the seabed, feed on seagrass or jellyfish and get rid of salt from their bodies by crying salty tears.

And turtles aren't the only oceanic reptiles — more than 60 species of snakes slither through the ocean. Their lungs reach almost to the end of their bodies, helping them hold their breath for two hours. Eight sea snake species must return to land to lay eggs. The rest stay at sea, where females give birth to live baby snakes. Like their land-based relatives, most sea snakes hunt with their venomous bite.

Olive ridley sea turtle

Kemp's ridley sea turtle

Yellow-bellied sea snake

Banded sea krait

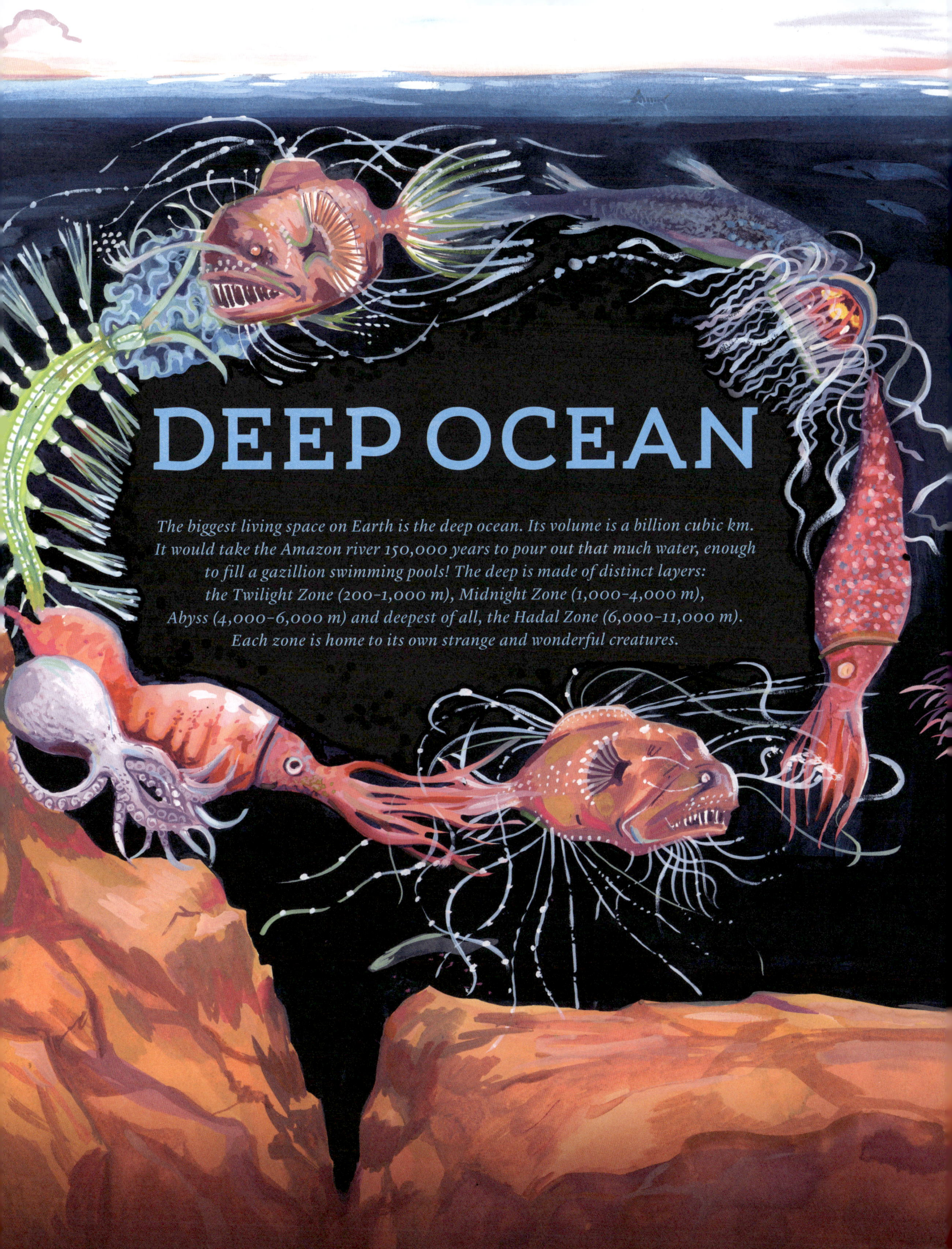

DEEP OCEAN

The biggest living space on Earth is the deep ocean. Its volume is a billion cubic km. It would take the Amazon river 150,000 years to pour out that much water, enough to fill a gazillion swimming pools! The deep is made of distinct layers: the Twilight Zone (200-1,000 m), Midnight Zone (1,000-4,000 m), Abyss (4,000-6,000 m) and deepest of all, the Hadal Zone (6,000-11,000 m). Each zone is home to its own strange and wonderful creatures.

STRAWBERRY SQUID

Histioteuthis heteropsis

Look into the eyes of a strawberry squid and you'll see something incredible. The right eye is small and the left eye is big. Strawberry squid have mismatched eyes and each one can look in a different direction at the same time.

These little squid are roughly the size of your hand, and they live in the shadowy waters of the Twilight Zone, some 1,000 m below the surface of the ocean. When scientists have filmed them using cameras on deep-diving robots, they've seen how strawberry squid use their amazing eyes. They hold their bodies at an angle so they can look upwards with their big eye and point their small eye downwards. Their big eye is good for seeing shadows of other animals passing overhead. The small eye is good for seeing flashes of light from glowing animals down in the dark depths below – some that the squid wants to eat, and others that want to eat the squid.

The strawberry squid is a perfect name because these animals really look like they're made out of strawberries. They have bright red skin that is covered in dots that look like strawberry seeds. In the deep ocean, the colour red looks dull, which helps the squid to hide. And the dots, called photophores, glow in the dark. Strawberry squid use their lights to startle predators and maybe to flash messages at other squid. So, these squid use their strawberry signals to talk to each other through the dark!

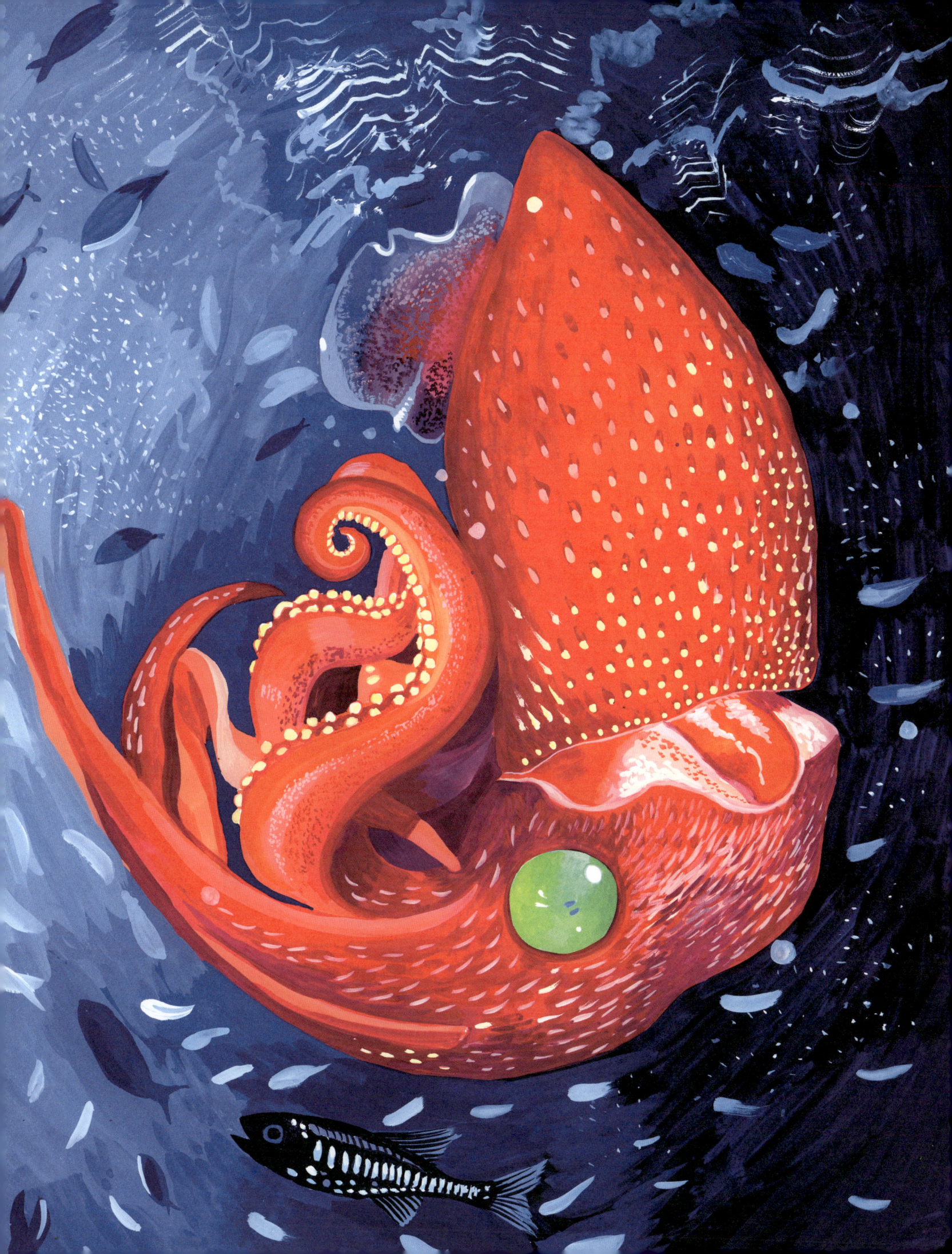

SWIMMING WORMS

Polychaetes

In gardens, parks and forests, the soil under your feet is full of wriggling worms. Worms also live in the deep ocean, where they dig and burrow in the seabed. And in the open waters of the Twilight and Midnight Zones live worms that do something completely different – they spend their whole lives swimming and drifting around.

It makes a lot of sense for deep-sea worms to learn to swim. Why let all that enormous space go to waste? To get there, they needed to evolve bodies that easily float. Jelly does the trick and lots of different worms have bodies filled with it.

Gossamer worms look like see-through centipedes. They shimmy their bodies and spin acrobatic loops. Like many deep-sea animals, gossamer worms can make their own light. When they get scared, they squirt golden sparkles into the water to distract an attacker while they escape into the darkness. Green bomber worms do a similar thing and chuck blobs of green light at intruders.

Whenever deep-sea scientists find swimming worms that nobody has seen before (which happens a lot), they need to decide what to call them. Sometimes the name is based on what the worms look like. Squid worms have long squiggly tentacles. Another type of worm is pink, round and has what looks like a little curling tail sticking out. Researchers couldn't resist naming this one the pig's butt worm! Whoever said scientists don't have a sense of humour?

PEARL OCTOPUSES

Muusoctopus robustus

Most octopuses are not very friendly towards each other. Usually they live on their own. But a few years ago, scientists were using a remote-controlled robot to study the deep sea off the California coast in the United States and they found something quite out of the ordinary. More than 3,000 m down in the Midnight Zone, near a giant underwater mountain, there were lots of pale purple octopuses sitting together on the seabed. Using their robot to take photographs, scientists worked out there were more than 20,000 octopuses! They called this special place the Octopus Garden.

All these visiting octopuses are females who are guarding their clutches of teardrop-shaped eggs, which they wrap up in their eight sucker-covered arms. They come to the Octopus Garden because warm water trickles through the seabed like a deep-sea jacuzzi. The warm water is around 10 °C, which makes their eggs grow five times faster than they would in the surrounding sea, which is a chilly 1.6 °C. But nothing happens quickly in the deep sea. It's almost two years before the baby octopuses at the Octopus Garden break out of their shells and swim off.

As happens in a lot of octopus species, after their eggs hatch, the mother pearl octopuses die. But their bodies provide important food for the ecosystem, including giant sea anemones. These relatives of jellyfish resemble flowers and their appearance make the Octopus Garden really look like a blooming garden.

Glow-in-the-Dark SHARKS

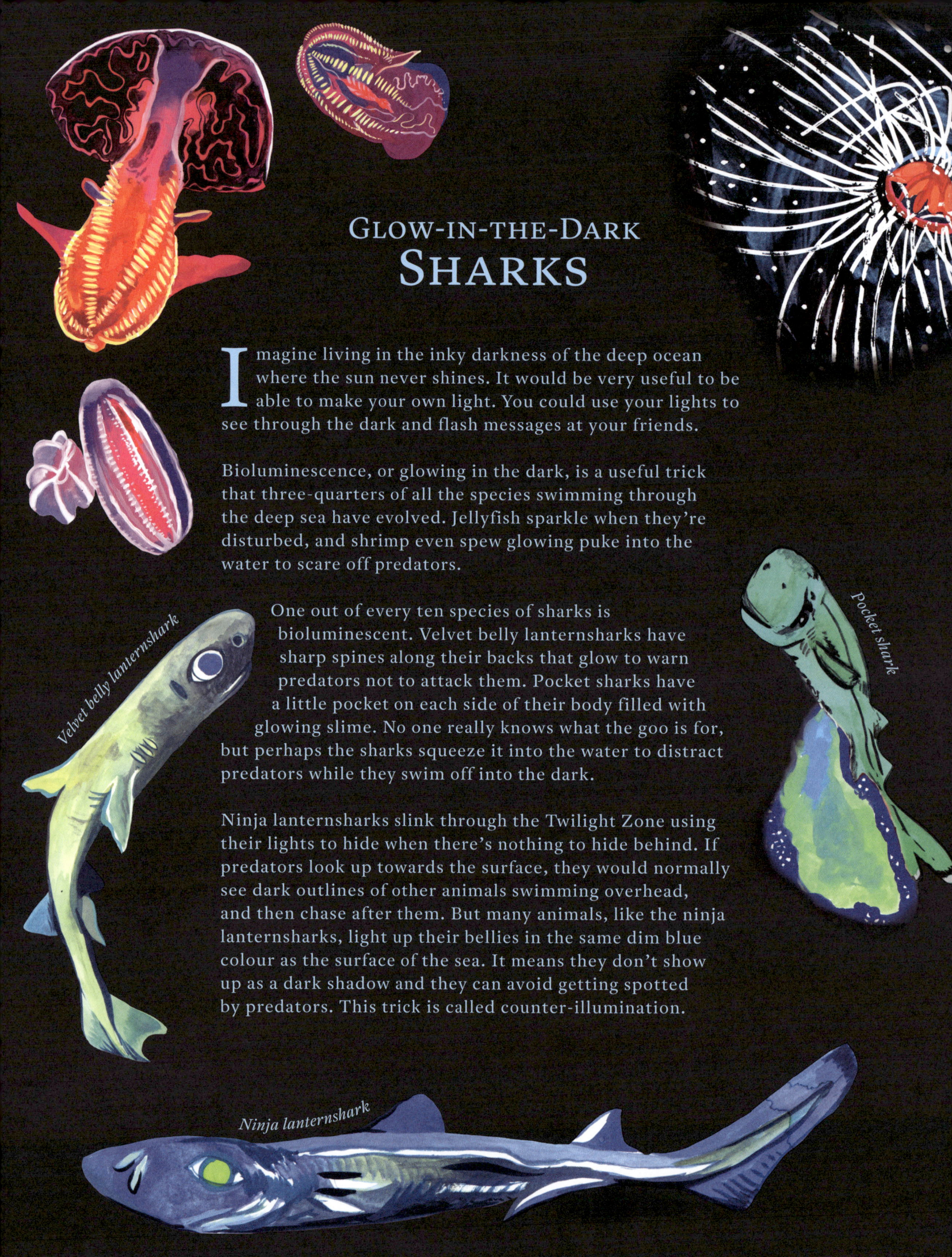

Imagine living in the inky darkness of the deep ocean where the sun never shines. It would be very useful to be able to make your own light. You could use your lights to see through the dark and flash messages at your friends.

Bioluminescence, or glowing in the dark, is a useful trick that three-quarters of all the species swimming through the deep sea have evolved. Jellyfish sparkle when they're disturbed, and shrimp even spew glowing puke into the water to scare off predators.

One out of every ten species of sharks is bioluminescent. Velvet belly lanternsharks have sharp spines along their backs that glow to warn predators not to attack them. Pocket sharks have a little pocket on each side of their body filled with glowing slime. No one really knows what the goo is for, but perhaps the sharks squeeze it into the water to distract predators while they swim off into the dark.

Ninja lanternsharks slink through the Twilight Zone using their lights to hide when there's nothing to hide behind. If predators look up towards the surface, they would normally see dark outlines of other animals swimming overhead, and then chase after them. But many animals, like the ninja lanternsharks, light up their bellies in the same dim blue colour as the surface of the sea. It means they don't show up as a dark shadow and they can avoid getting spotted by predators. This trick is called counter-illumination.

Velvet belly lanternshark

Pocket shark

Ninja lanternshark

Kitefin shark

Fanfin angler

Anglerfish

The biggest glowing sharks are kitefin sharks. They swim very slowly just above the seabed and their shining bellies act like searchlights helping them spot prey.

Deep-sea animals can make themselves glow in two ways. Some make chemicals in their bodies, which produce light when mixed together. Other animals have glowing bacteria living inside them. Flashlight fish have a pouch under each eye filled with bioluminescent bacteria that help them see through the dark, like a car's headlights. Anglerfish have bacteria at the end of a prong sticking out of their foreheads, which they use to tempt prey towards their huge jaws.

Blue and green are the most common colours that animals glow. A few make yellow light and the rarest colour is red. Most deep-sea animals can't see red light. One fish, the stoplight loosejaw, not only sees red light but also makes it. This gives them a secret way of seeing through the dark without anything else seeing them. So, even though the sun never shines that far down, the deep sea is not completely dark.

Flashlight fish

Stoplight loosejaw

FANFIN ANGLERS

Caulophryne jordani

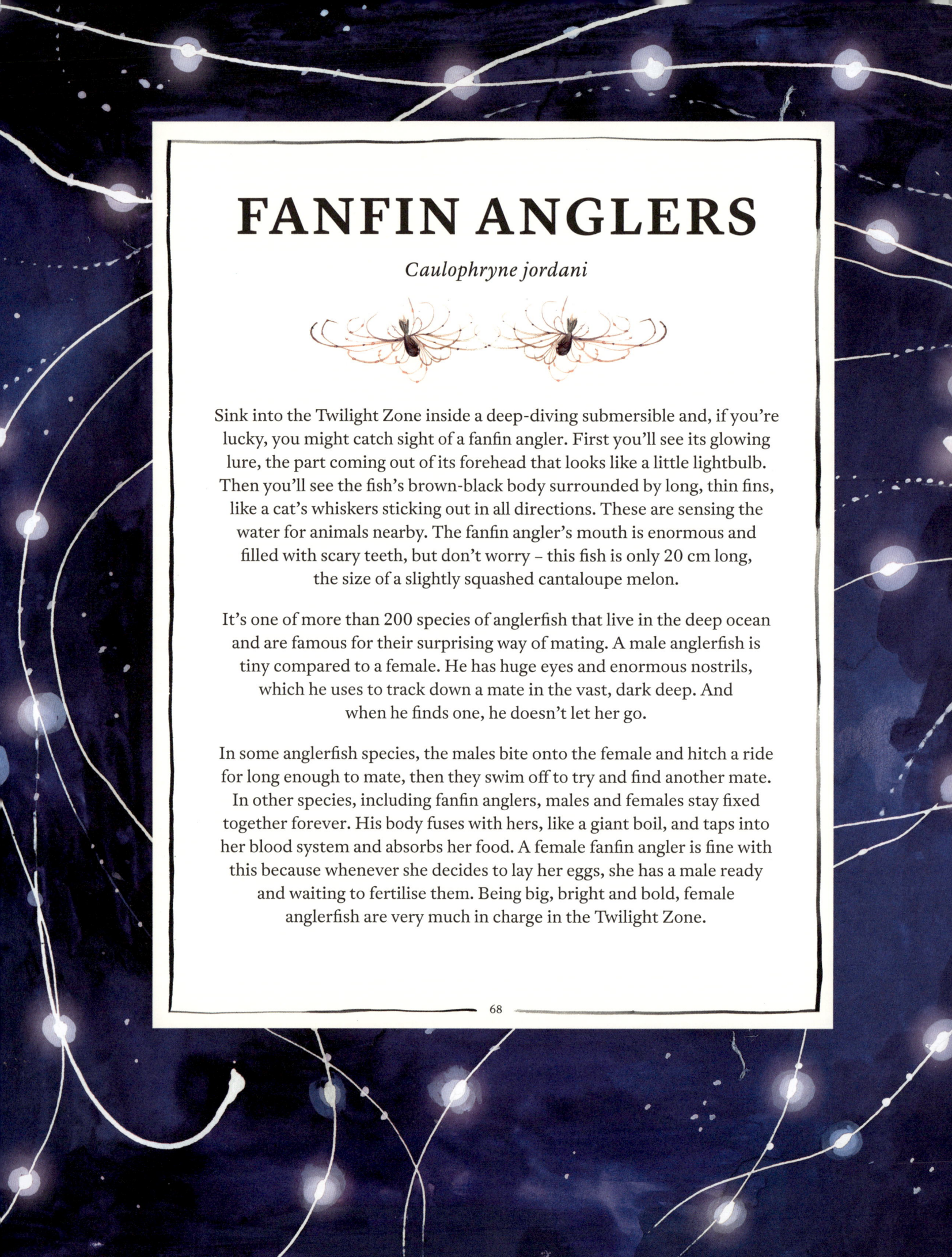

Sink into the Twilight Zone inside a deep-diving submersible and, if you're lucky, you might catch sight of a fanfin angler. First you'll see its glowing lure, the part coming out of its forehead that looks like a little lightbulb. Then you'll see the fish's brown-black body surrounded by long, thin fins, like a cat's whiskers sticking out in all directions. These are sensing the water for animals nearby. The fanfin angler's mouth is enormous and filled with scary teeth, but don't worry – this fish is only 20 cm long, the size of a slightly squashed cantaloupe melon.

It's one of more than 200 species of anglerfish that live in the deep ocean and are famous for their surprising way of mating. A male anglerfish is tiny compared to a female. He has huge eyes and enormous nostrils, which he uses to track down a mate in the vast, dark deep. And when he finds one, he doesn't let her go.

In some anglerfish species, the males bite onto the female and hitch a ride for long enough to mate, then they swim off to try and find another mate. In other species, including fanfin anglers, males and females stay fixed together forever. His body fuses with hers, like a giant boil, and taps into her blood system and absorbs her food. A female fanfin angler is fine with this because whenever she decides to lay her eggs, she has a male ready and waiting to fertilise them. Being big, bright and bold, female anglerfish are very much in charge in the Twilight Zone.

PSYCHEDELIC JELLYFISH

Crossota millsae

Swimming in the Midnight Zone are thumb-sized creatures called psychedelic jellyfish. Their bodies are dome-shaped like smooth umbrellas and coloured ruby red, orange and purple. They have masses of stinging tentacles, which they can hold out straight or curl up into springs or fold neatly under their umbrella.

When it comes to reproducing, in most types of jellyfish the females release eggs into the water and males release sperm to fertilise them. The fertilised eggs then turn into jellyfish larvae, which drift off and never see their parents again. Psychedelic jellyfish do things differently. The females hold on to their eggs and let the babies grow up under the protective umbrella of their bodies. The babies even sprout little tentacles and start eating some of their mother's food. Eventually, they're ready to swim off and start living on their own.

Lots of creatures that look like jellyfish are actually different types of closely related animals. (And they are definitely not fish, which is why some people prefer calling them jellies). There are 'true' jellyfish, such as moon jellyfish and lion's mane jellyfish. Stalked jellyfish grow on the seabed and box jellyfish have square-shaped bodies. Psychedelic jellyfish belong to a related group of animals called hydrozoans. And there are much more distant relatives, comb jellies, which look like alien spaceships gliding through the deep ocean. Even though their bodies are made mostly of water, it's amazing what jellyfish get up to, especially the ones down in the deep sea!

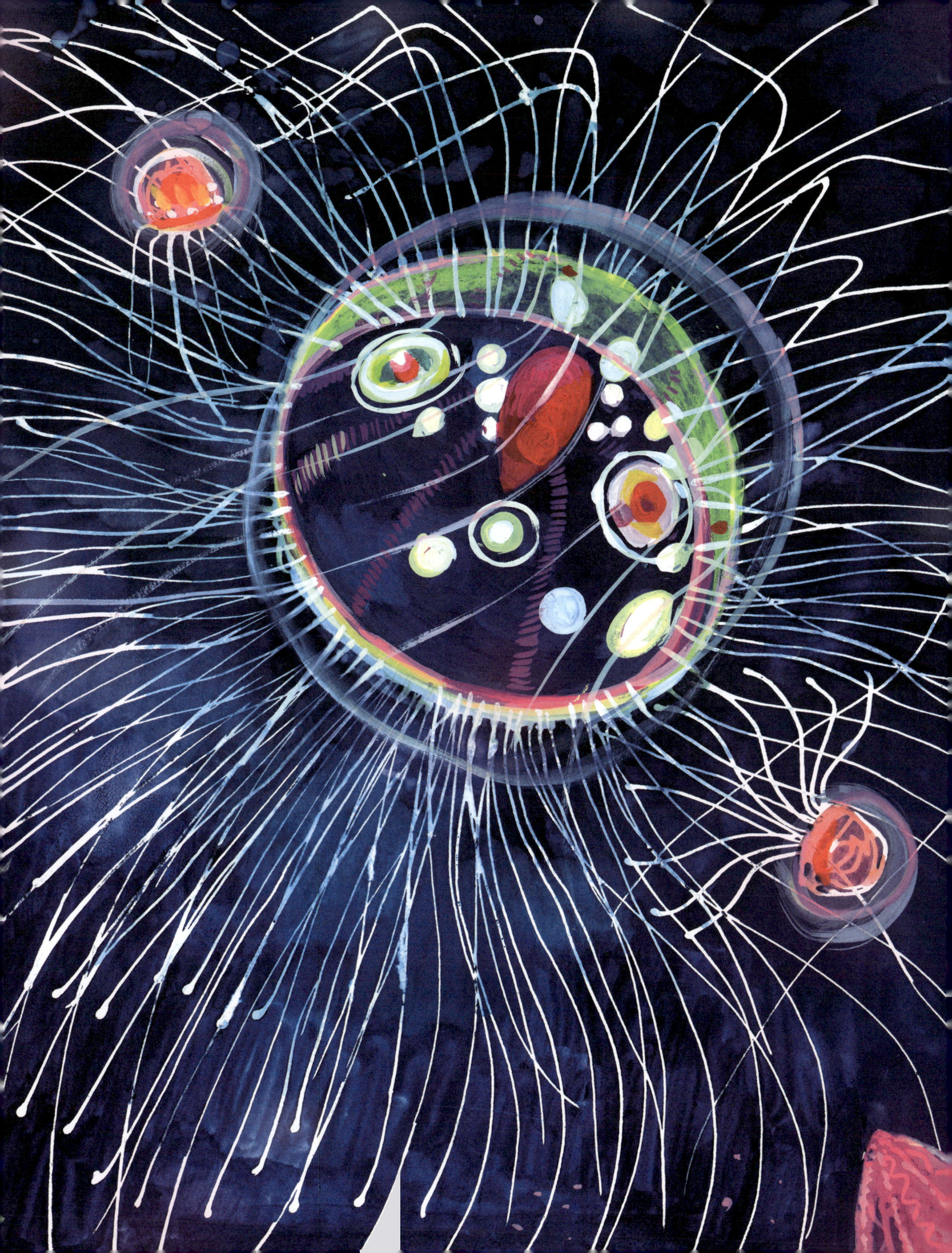

Life All the Way Down

Less than 200 years ago, most scientists thought that nothing lived in the deep ocean. They thought it was too cold and dark, there wasn't enough food and the pressure was far too high for anything to survive there. At the time they didn't have very good equipment to study the deep ocean. Now there are high-tech deep-diving robots that scientists can use to search the deep, and submersibles they can climb inside to go there themselves. And they've seen that there's life all the way to the very bottom.

Dumbo octopuses are swimming around 7,000 m down, using flaps in the sides of their bodies that look like big ears. At more than 8,000 m down, there are pink, pudgy snailfish that are unaffected by the crushing pressure. There are even animals living more than 10 km down at the bottom of the Mariana Trench. Sea cucumbers, jellyfish and crustaceans called amphipods are among the deepest of all animals on Earth. Weird things called xenophyophores also live down there. Each one is made from a single, giant cell about 10 cm across (your body is made of trillions of microscopic cells).

Crushing pressure is just part of everyday life for deep-sea animals. Many of them are so used to it, they actually need the high pressure to survive. When scientists bring

Pelican eel

Black swallower

Vampire squid

Osedax

them to the surface to study them, these creatures come up in bad shape — if a dinnerplate jellyfish is brought to the surface, its body completely falls apart.

There's not much food in the deep ocean and animals can't be fussy. Lots of deep-sea fish have enormous mouths and super-stretchy stomachs so they can gulp down prey, no matter how big it is. Pelican eels have jaws that unfold like an umbrella, and black swallowers have stomachs like balloons that can fit other fish twice as long as they are. An important source of food in the deep ocean are fluffy white specks that drift down from the surface, called marine snow. This stuff is not as nice as it sounds. It's made of dead phytoplankton and zooplankton and their poos, all stuck together with goo. But in the deep sea, food is food! Animals such as vampire squid gather marine snow as it falls. Sea cucumbers and starfish eat marine snow that piles up on the seabed.

When large dead animals fall into the deep sea, they don't go to waste. One whale provides enough food for thousands of animals for several decades, including species that only eat one particular part of these dead giants. *Osedax* are worms that look like plants with green roots. They wait for scavengers to pick a whale's skeleton clean, then move in and eat the whale's bare bones.

Life in the deepest parts of the ocean is only for the hardiest creatures. Could you take the pressure?

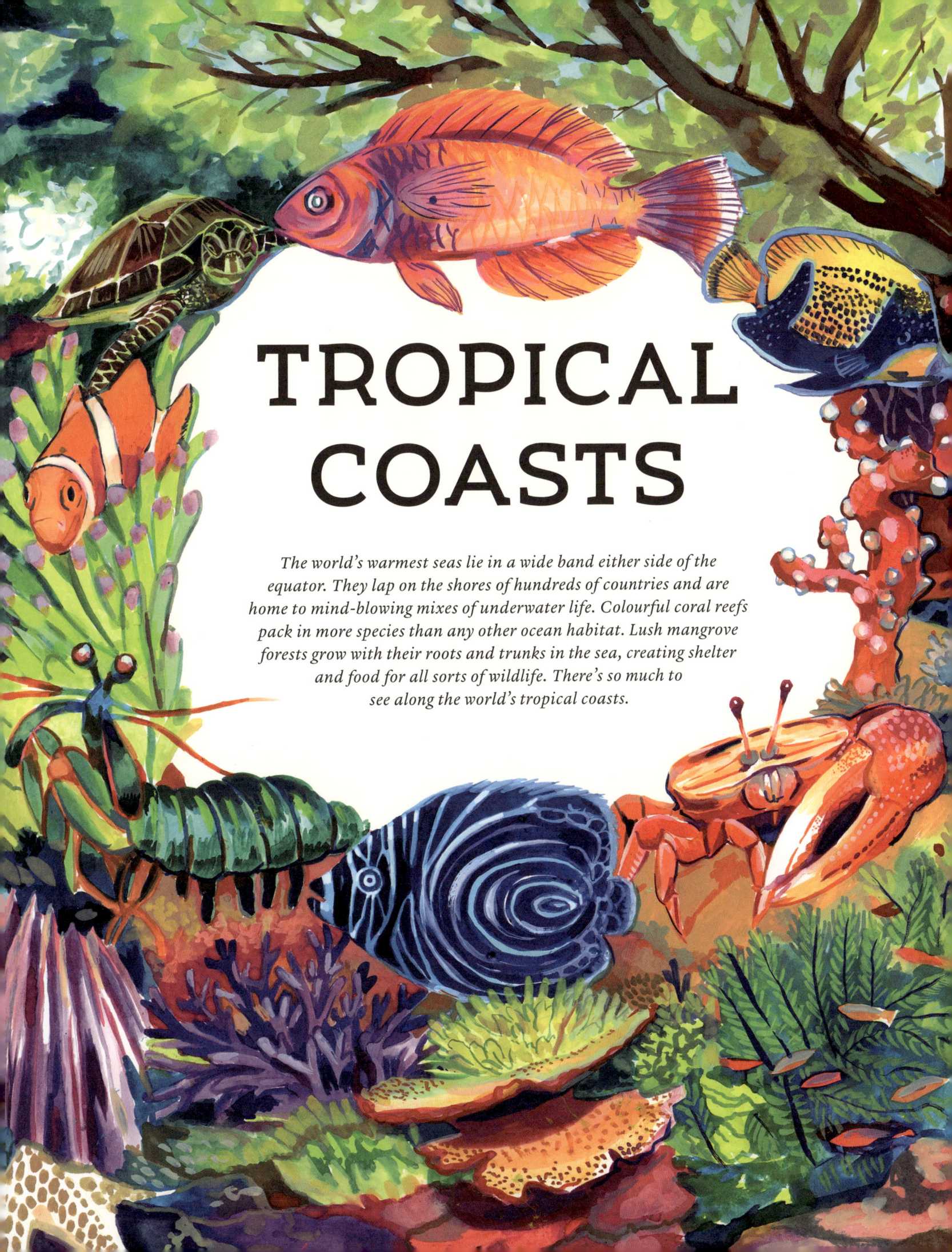

TROPICAL COASTS

The world's warmest seas lie in a wide band either side of the equator. They lap on the shores of hundreds of countries and are home to mind-blowing mixes of underwater life. Colourful coral reefs pack in more species than any other ocean habitat. Lush mangrove forests grow with their roots and trunks in the sea, creating shelter and food for all sorts of wildlife. There's so much to see along the world's tropical coasts.

ROSE-VEILED FAIRY WRASSE

Cirrhilabrus finifenmaa

To explore coral reefs in shallow tropical seas, divers breathing air from scuba tanks can stay down for an hour or so and safely reach 30 m underwater. But there's much more to coral reefs. Using special equipment, divers can now go much deeper for much longer. Instead of blowing air bubbles into the water, they rebreathe the same air again and again, with extra oxygen added from a small tank. This lets them explore reefs that used to be out of reach and find species nobody knew about before – such as the rose-veiled fairy wrasse.

These little fish live around the islands of the Maldives and Sri Lanka 70 m underwater. They are very beautiful with rosy pink heads. Scientists call them *finifenmaa*, which means 'rose' in the local Dhivehi language in the Maldives. This group of fish are known as fairies because they are small and colourful.

The males are the most gorgeous and use their colours to attract females. And like many other fish, rose-veiled fairy wrasse change the way they look and change their sex as they get older. They start life as less colourful females, then later they switch roles and become glamorous males. Even little fish like to make themselves look pretty!

Fish Are SMART

It's a puzzling sight on a coral reef to see small, stripy fish dart across the bodies of bigger fish and even swim right inside their huge open mouths past rows of sharp teeth. What are these little fish thinking, putting themselves in such danger? You might wonder if they're stupid, but even though their brains are small, these fish are very clever! Cleaner wrasse, as they're known, understand that bigger fish need them to stay clean and healthy. Big fish arrive at a cleaner wrasse's cleaning station, like people driving to a car wash. When their turn comes, the big fish hold still while the cleaner wrasse removes dead skin from their bodies and picks off bloodsucking parasites.

Every day, hundreds of fish visit a cleaning station run by one or two cleaner wrasse that remember every single one of their visitors. The wrasse learn which fish are dangerous predators, such as groupers or moray eels, and treat them with the greatest care. They only eat parasites and never sneak a tasty bite of living skin, or they could get snapped up inside a pair of angry jaws. Cleaner wrasse can somehow tell when a predator hasn't eaten in a while — all the more reason to provide an extra-good service so they don't become its next meal.

When a harmless fish comes along, like a seaweed-nibbling rabbitfish, the cleaner wrasse know they can be naughty. They might take a bite of living skin, which gives the rabbitfish a

sharp nip. The wrasse rubs and smooths over the annoyed rabbitfish, which clearly enjoys the feeling because they stick around and don't swim off in a huff.

How can we tell that cleaner wrasse are so clever? Scientists think they may even recognise their reflection in a mirror, which is a sign of intelligence. Often animals think their reflection is another animal and try to attack it or run away. But cleaner wrasse, like some other smart animals such as elephants and crows, peer closely and perhaps realise that they are looking at themselves in the mirror. And cleaner wrasse aren't the only smart fish. Sharks have good memories. Sticklebacks can count. And archerfish solve complicated mathematical problems to help them hunt!

Among the roots of mangrove trees, archerfish search for insects sitting on twigs and leaves overhanging the water. When they spot a target, the underwater hunter shoots a mouthful of water into the air like a bullet. They use their inbuilt maths skills to work out exactly how far, how high and what angle they need to fire in order to knock an insect off its perch. Then the archerfish darts underneath and waits in just the right spot to gobble up their prey when it plops into the water. So never underestimate a fish – it could be a secret genius!

PEACOCK MANTIS SHRIMP

Odontodactylus scyllarus

Brightly coloured and roughly the size of a banana, peacock mantis shrimps are a dazzling sight on coral reefs. But don't be distracted by their good looks – they are ferocious predators! Mantis shrimps hold the world record for the strongest punch of any animal – even stronger than a kangaroo or a gorilla! They can shoot out their claws at 23 m per second, fifty times faster than a blink of an eye. If people keep them in aquariums, mantis shrimps can escape by smashing the glass to pieces.

They use a pair of front claws, known as dactyls, to smash snails, crabs and clams. A shrimp's muscles pull on part of the leg, bending it like an archer drawing back a bow and arrow. Then the shrimp releases the leg and sends it smashing into its prey. This happens so fast it creates tiny bubbles that heat up to the temperature of the sun when they pop!

Mantis shrimp also have incredible eyes. Human eyes usually have three types of receptors that together can sense the colours of the rainbow. Mantis shrimp have an incredible 12 types of receptors for seeing colours. They can also see in ultraviolet light, or UV, which is invisible to people. Can you imagine what the world looks like to a fast-punching mantis shrimp?

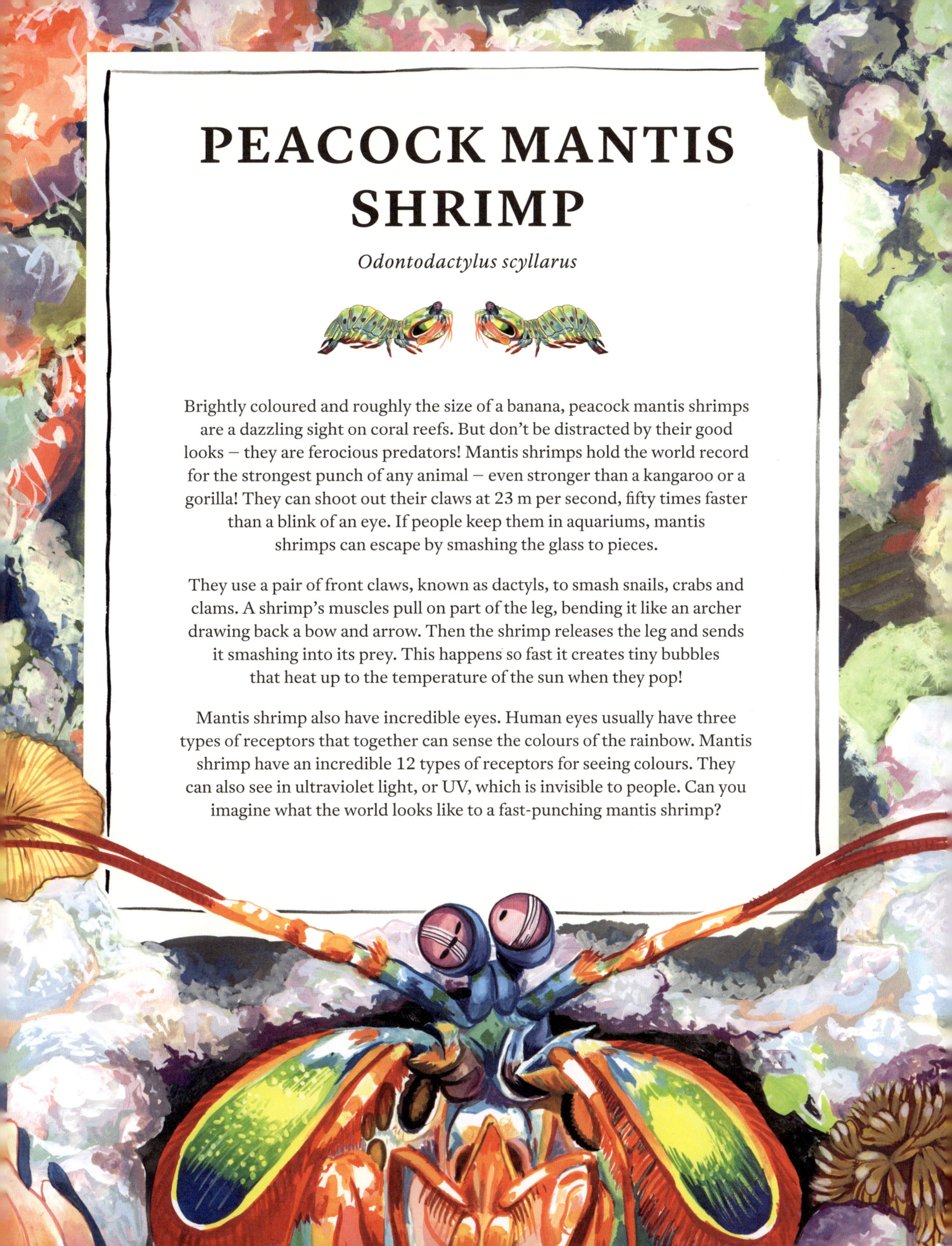

ANGELFISH

Pomacanthus

Angelfish are often the easiest fish to spot on a bustling coral reef. They are big and brightly coloured, and while other animals prefer to hide away in nooks in the reef or blend with their surroundings, angelfish are usually bold and parade around in ones or twos.

With their flamboyant colours and patterns, angelfish announce who they are to everyone else on the reef. 'I am a blueface angelfish,' yell the fish with yellow bodies covered in honeycomb patterns and shining blue scribbles across their faces. 'We are emperor angelfish,' shout the fish with canary yellow and midnight blue stripes. 'We are blue ring angelfish,' say the fish with shining blue circles across their dark bodies. The true meaning of these messages is clear to other angelfish: 'Stay away!' Angelfish are highly territorial and claim parts of the reef as their own. They don't want other angelfish of the same species coming near and eating the sponges and sea squirts or stealing their mates.

Young angelfish look completely different to the adults. When they're small, many of these species are difficult to tell apart. They are all dark-coloured and have blue and white stripes across their bodies. These colours are like a school uniform. They show the adult fish that they are still only young and don't plan to steal their territory . . . well, not just yet!

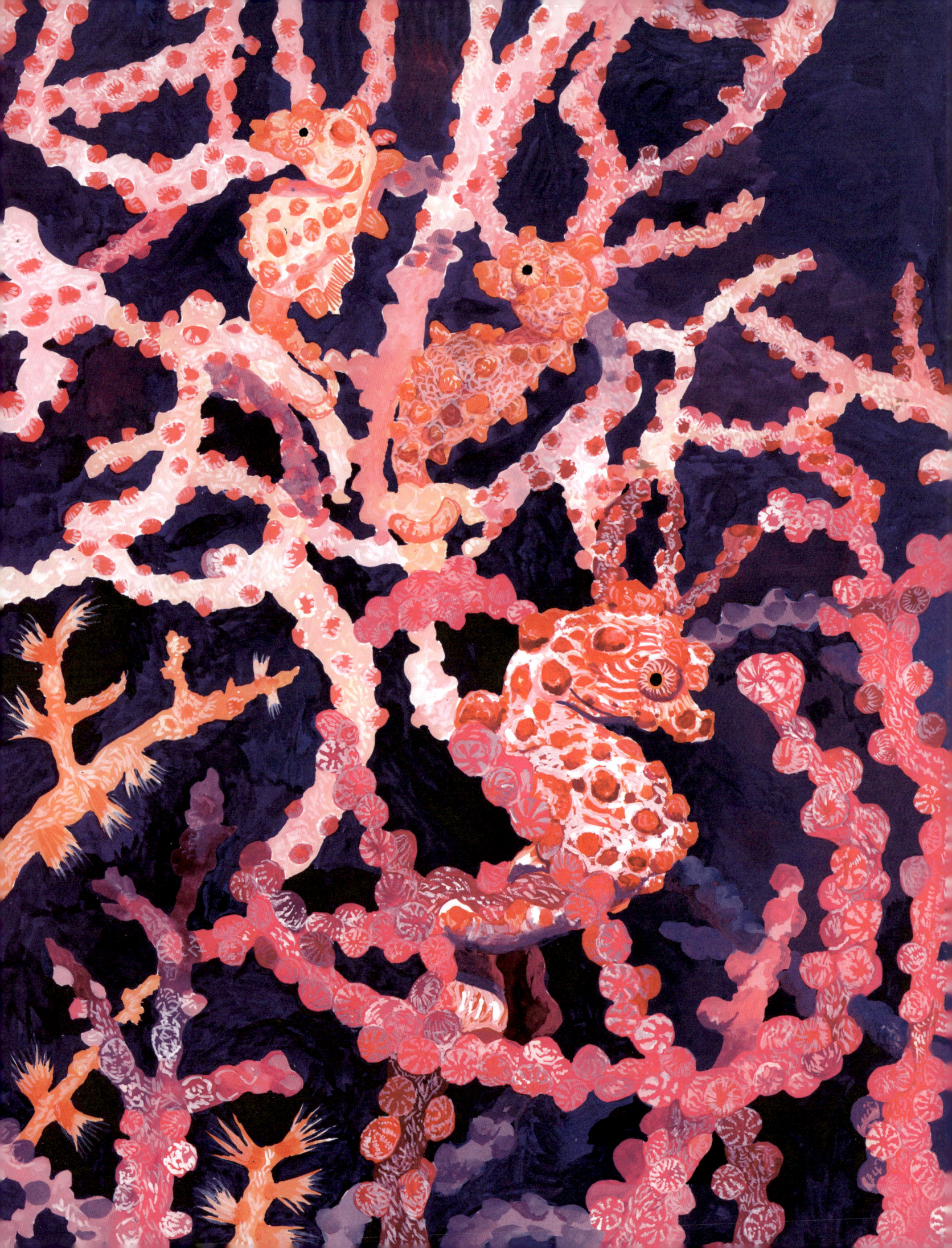

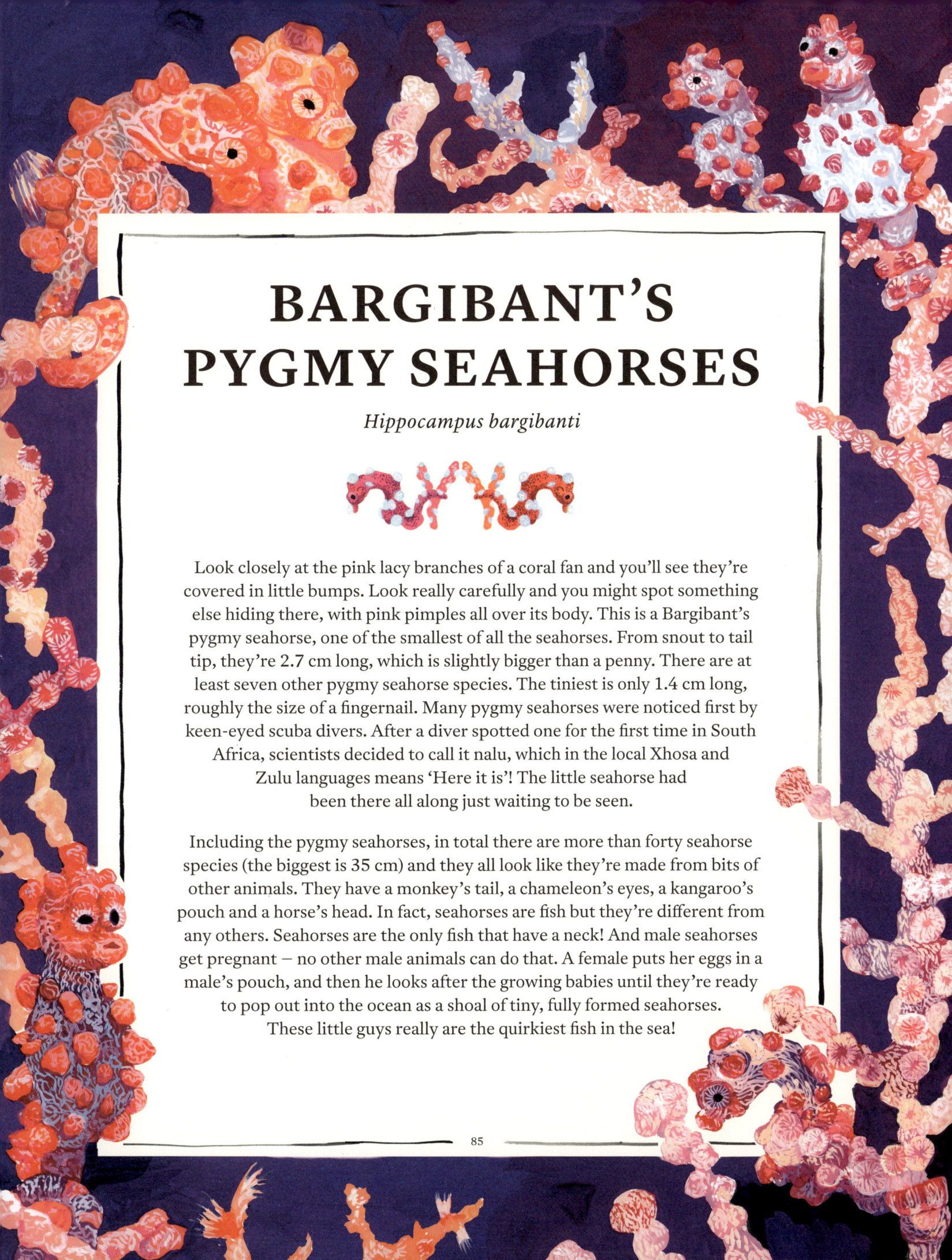

BARGIBANT'S PYGMY SEAHORSES

Hippocampus bargibanti

Look closely at the pink lacy branches of a coral fan and you'll see they're covered in little bumps. Look really carefully and you might spot something else hiding there, with pink pimples all over its body. This is a Bargibant's pygmy seahorse, one of the smallest of all the seahorses. From snout to tail tip, they're 2.7 cm long, which is slightly bigger than a penny. There are at least seven other pygmy seahorse species. The tiniest is only 1.4 cm long, roughly the size of a fingernail. Many pygmy seahorses were noticed first by keen-eyed scuba divers. After a diver spotted one for the first time in South Africa, scientists decided to call it nalu, which in the local Xhosa and Zulu languages means 'Here it is'! The little seahorse had been there all along just waiting to be seen.

Including the pygmy seahorses, in total there are more than forty seahorse species (the biggest is 35 cm) and they all look like they're made from bits of other animals. They have a monkey's tail, a chameleon's eyes, a kangaroo's pouch and a horse's head. In fact, seahorses are fish but they're different from any others. Seahorses are the only fish that have a neck! And male seahorses get pregnant – no other male animals can do that. A female puts her eggs in a male's pouch, and then he looks after the growing babies until they're ready to pop out into the ocean as a shoal of tiny, fully formed seahorses. These little guys really are the quirkiest fish in the sea!

CORAL REEF Teams

Coral reefs are like bustling cities. Masses of different creatures live in a scrambling, mingling mix. Every tiny space on a reef has something growing on it or swimming past. If you set out to count all the living species in the seas, you would find that one in every four comes from a coral reef. To share these busy spaces, lots of reef species have learned to work together – including the animals that build the solid parts of the reefs.

Even though they look like colourful rocks, reefs are built by corals, which are a team of animals and algae. The animal parts are the corals, which are close relatives of jellyfish and sea anemones. Each chunk of coral is made from thousands of tiny creatures called polyps, which have tentacles that look like flower petals. The coral polyps nestle inside little cups made of a tough material called calcium carbonate (or chalk). If you look at a polyp under a microscope, you'll see millions of tiny green and brown blobs. These are mini algae called zooxanthellae, or zoox. Coral polyps and zoox work together as a team. Zoox are like plants and use the sun's energy to make sugars to feed themselves, and the corals too. In return, corals give zoox somewhere safe to live where there's plenty of sunshine to grow.

Coral polyps

When different types of creatures team up, it's called symbiosis. Animals on coral reefs strike up partnerships and share their special skills. Pistol shrimp dig burrows in the sandy seabed near coral reefs. They use their front claws to push out the sand and keep the burrow clean and tidy. But they can't see far, which is why they don't live alone. Each shrimp's burrow is also home to a goby, a little fish with good eyesight. The goby sits at the burrow entrance watching out for danger. If a predator comes near, the goby darts into the burrow and the shrimp does too.

Clownfish live in symbiosis with sea anemones. These orange and white striped fish shelter among the anemone's stinging tentacles and you'll never see one living anywhere else. Scientists think a layer of slime over the clownfish's bodies stops them getting stung. Meanwhile, anemones do better when they have fish living with them. The clownfish chase off butterflyfish that try to nip the anemone's tentacles. And at night, clownfish wriggle around, bringing in fresh water, which helps the anemone breathe and grow. There's also a third member of this team. Living inside the anemone are tiny zoox, which make sugars to feed the anemone. Clownfish play their part, helping the zoox to grow by fertilising them with their wee. On a busy coral reef, there are lots of ways of being a good neighbour!

MAGNIFICENT FRIGATEBIRDS

Fregata magnificens

The breeding season is a noisy and colourful time for magnificent frigatebirds. As many as thirty males perch together in the branches of a mangrove tree and show off to females flying by. They inflate a huge, bright red balloon on their throat called a gular pouch. They spread their wide, shiny black wings, make a drumming sound by vibrating their red throat balloons and clack their bills. When a female picks a mate, the pair perform a courtship dance, nodding their heads and weaving their necks together. Then comes the important business of rearing a chick. In a nest made of twigs, a female frigatebird lays a single egg that takes almost two months to hatch.

To catch food for themselves and their hungry chicks, the magnificent frigatebird parents soar over the sea and dip down for fish and shrimp, but they mustn't get too wet because their feathers are not waterproof and they can't fly if they get soaking and salty. A nickname for them is 'pirate birds' because they sometimes steal food from other birds. They grab and shake the tail feathers of tropicbirds and boobies, forcing them to throw up the food they've just eaten. The pirate then swoops in and catches the ejected meal in mid-air. That's a clever, but rather disgusting, way to feed your family!

FIDDLER CRABS

Ocypodidae

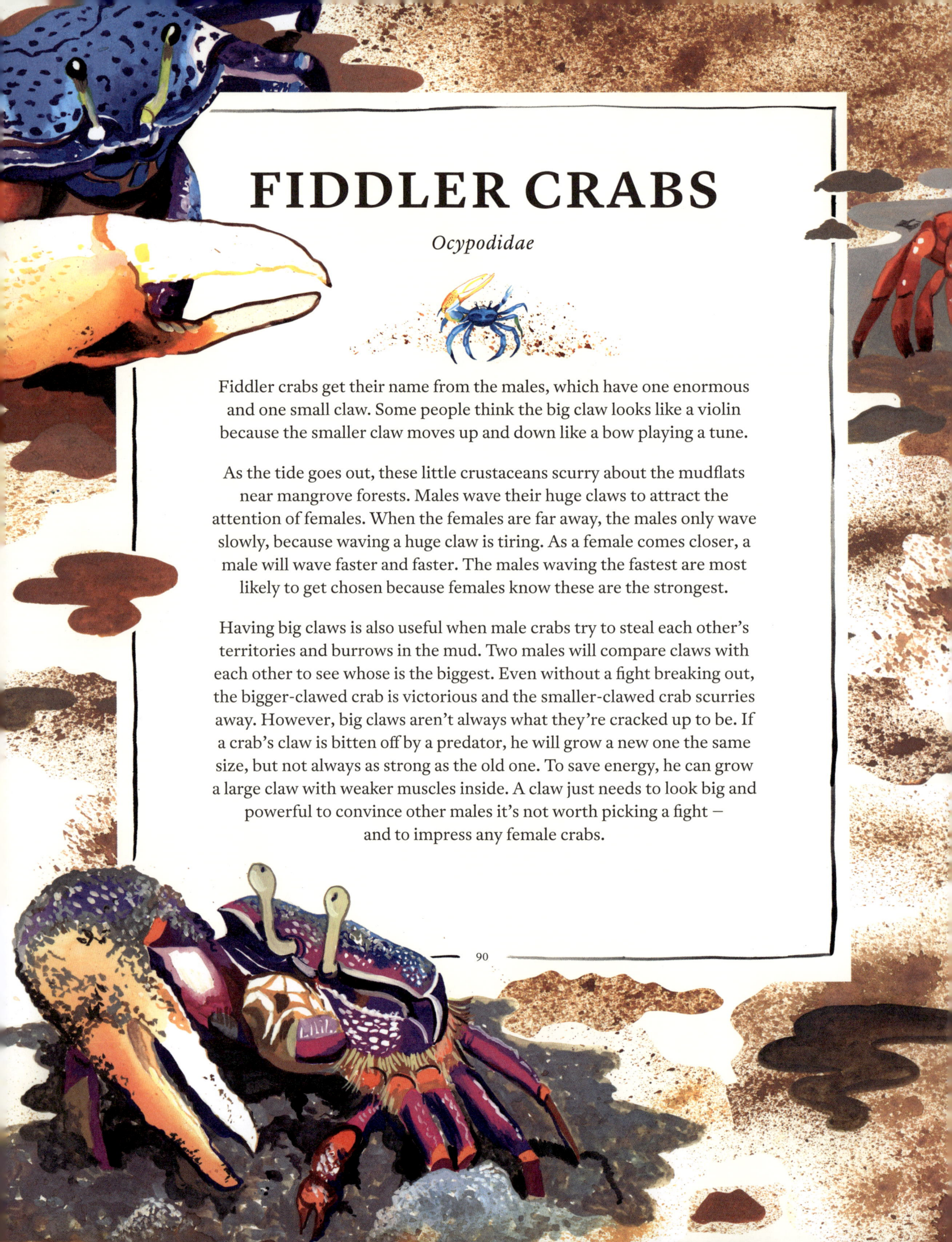

Fiddler crabs get their name from the males, which have one enormous and one small claw. Some people think the big claw looks like a violin because the smaller claw moves up and down like a bow playing a tune.

As the tide goes out, these little crustaceans scurry about the mudflats near mangrove forests. Males wave their huge claws to attract the attention of females. When the females are far away, the males only wave slowly, because waving a huge claw is tiring. As a female comes closer, a male will wave faster and faster. The males waving the fastest are most likely to get chosen because females know these are the strongest.

Having big claws is also useful when male crabs try to steal each other's territories and burrows in the mud. Two males will compare claws with each other to see whose is the biggest. Even without a fight breaking out, the bigger-clawed crab is victorious and the smaller-clawed crab scurries away. However, big claws aren't always what they're cracked up to be. If a crab's claw is bitten off by a predator, he will grow a new one the same size, but not always as strong as the old one. To save energy, he can grow a large claw with weaker muscles inside. A claw just needs to look big and powerful to convince other males it's not worth picking a fight — and to impress any female crabs.

Our Changing OCEAN

For hundreds of millions of years, the ocean has been full of incredible living things — but it hasn't always been the same. All sorts of animals used to roam the ocean that aren't there today. Long ago, masses of trilobites were scuttling across the seabed and swimming through the seas. There were more than 25,000 species of trilobites (and just think, there were only around 1,000 species of dinosaurs!). There used to be weird relatives of sharks in the sea that looked like they had a toothbrush stuck on their head or a toothy spiral in their mouth. And of course, there were giant swimming reptiles, like ichthyosaurs and plesiosaurs. Today, you won't spot any of these animals prowling the ocean.

In the past, the ocean has been much hotter and also much colder than it is now, and sea levels have risen and fallen. When it was colder, there was more ice and less liquid water and so the sea level dropped. When it was warmer, ice melted and the sea level went up.

All of these changes happened long before people came along. Sadly, the ocean is now changing fast because of things people are doing. Some animals are vanishing from the ocean because people are catching too many of them. Enormous fishing boats tow huge nets or fishing lines more than 80 km long and covered in thousands of hooks. This doesn't only catch fish that people will eat, but other animals like sharks and sea turtles that get thrown back into the sea, usually already dead.

Rubbish and pollution end up in the ocean. Trillions of specks of plastic are floating in the sea that have broken down from bigger things such as plastic bottles. Chemicals made by people wash into the seas and poison wildlife. And because of greenhouse gases, the ocean is getting warmer and warmer. Many species are too hot, so they're moving to try and find cooler water. Habitats, like coral reefs and seagrass meadows, suffer when heatwaves strike and parts of the ocean suddenly get much hotter.

The good news is that the ocean and its amazing wildlife can recover and be healthier – we just need to give a helping hand. People can protect more species and habitats inside marine reserves, where no fishing is allowed. People can stop making and using so much plastic and toxic chemicals. People can fish in more sustainable ways, using equipment that doesn't kill other animals or damage the seabed. And people can stop burning so much fossil fuel and switch to alternatives like wind turbines and solar panels, which don't release greenhouse gases.

Most of all, we can all care about the ocean, learn more about it and share stories with other people about all the incredible things that live there.

GLOSSARY

antarctica
The continent that surrounds Earth's South Pole. It is almost completely covered in ice.

antennae (singular: antenna)
The two long, thin 'feelers' on the heads of insects, crustaceans and other animals, used for touching and smelling.

antidote
A chemical substance that works to counter the dangerous effects of some poisons, such as snake venom.

Arctic
The North Pole and the area around it. The Arctic is the northernmost region of Earth.

baleen plates
In place of teeth, stiff bristly structures made of keratin (the same substance that makes up hair and nails) inside the jaws of some whales, used for sifting small prey from seawater.

bioluminescence
A chemical reaction inside a living organism that produces a light that can glow, twinkle or pulsate. Light can also be created by bacteria living on the organism's skin. Many jellyfish are bioluminescent.

blubber
A thick layer of fat under the skin of many marine animals, including whales, seals and walruses. Blubber keeps these animals warm in cold waters.

coral reefs
Underwater structures made up of the skeletons of hard coral – small colourful marine animals. They mostly grow in warm, tropical waters.

crustaceans
Invertebrates (animals without a backbone) with hard coverings on the outside of their bodies called exoskeletons. Crabs, shrimps and lobsters are all crustaceans.

currents
The continuous flow of water in the ocean. Currents can flow across the sea surface, through the deep sea or up and down.

echinoderm
A group of marine animals that live on the ocean floor. All echinoderms have radial symmetry, which means their arms all come out from one central point. Starfish are echinoderms.

ecosystem
A community of living and non-living things (such as weather and soil) that share a natural environment and interact and rely on each other for survival.

equator
The imaginary circle that runs around Earth, dividing it into the Northern Hemisphere and the Southern Hemisphere.

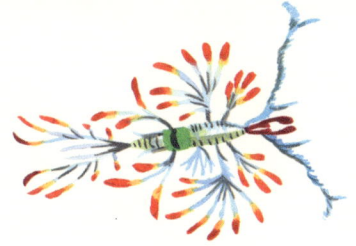

gills
Organs used by fish and some other underwater animals for breathing. Gills extract the oxygen from water.

greenhouse gases
Natural gases in the Earth's atmosphere, such as carbon dioxide and methane, that trap heat. The more of these gases we humans release into our atmosphere by burning fossil fuels, the hotter our planet gets.

larvae (singular: larva)
The early stages of some species' life (including fish, crabs and starfish) after they have hatched from an egg.

mantle
The sack-like part of an octopus or squid that houses all its vital organs.

marine
Relating to or found in the sea.

microscopic
Something that is too small to see with the human eye.

mollusc
Invertebrates with soft bodies. An octopus is a mollusc.

parasites
Animals or plants that live on or inside another organism to feed on it.

pods
Family groups of whales or dolphins, that hunt and travel together, as well as protect each other.

predator
An animal that hunts and eats other animals.

reptile
Cold-blooded animals with scaly skin. Snakes and turtles are reptiles.

shoal
A large group of fish swimming together.

symbiosis
A close relationship in nature between two different species, which is helpful for them both.

tentacles
Long, flexible body parts on sea animals such as corals, squid and jellyfish, used to grab and sting things around them.

A FINAL NOTE FROM THE AUTHOR

We've reached the end of our journey around the world's ocean and met all sorts of wonderful wildlife along the way. We've dipped our toes in freezing polar seas, explored the coasts, sailed offshore to the wide-open seas and plunged into the deep. We've seen the biggest fish and the smallest plankton. We've watched squid fly and sharks glow in the dark.

Did you have a favourite species or a favourite place? Or are you like me and find it impossible to choose between all the amazing things that live in the ocean? These are just a few of the many, many marine species we know of. No one knows for sure how many there are in total in the ocean because we haven't found them all yet – there could be millions! As people keep going out and exploring more of the ocean, they are seeing more creatures that nobody has spotted before and learning more about this huge, important part of our planet.
What do you think they will find next?